KU-191-817

THE WISDOM OF THE EAST SERIES

EDITED BY J. L. CRANMER-BYNG, M.C.

PERSIAN PROVERBS

Persian Proverbs

by

L. P. ELWELL-SUTTON, B.A.
Lecturer in Persian,
University of Edinburgh

John Murray, Albemarle Street,
London, W.

First Edition . . . 1954

Printed in Great Britain by Butler & Tanner Ltd., Frome and London
and Published by John Murray (Publishers) Ltd.

CONTENTS

EDITORIAL NOTE

THE object of the Editor of this series is a very definite one. He desires above all things that these books shall be the ambassadors of good-will between East and West. He hopes that they will contribute to a fuller knowledge of the great cultural heritage of the East, for only through real understanding will the West be able to appreciate the underlying problems and aspirations of Asia to-day. He is confident that a deeper knowledge of the great ideals and lofty philosophy of Eastern thought will help to a revival of that true spirit of charity which neither despises nor fears the nations of another creed and colour.

J. L. CRANMER-BYNG.

50, ALBEMARLE STREET,
LONDON, W.1.

INTRODUCTION

Popular folk-lore has long since emerged from the contempt in which it was formerly held by men of letters. Even in the East, where classical literary standards still hold universal sway, the more progressive writers are beginning to explore the wealth hidden in this field and to realize that the pithy and pungent mode of expression of the common people, their vividness and directness of imagination, can add something to an author's work that he can never get from imitation of the old models.

Proverbs contain the essence of this popular wisdom, and even the small collection presented in this book is sufficient to paint a lively picture of Persian life and character. It is of course a Persia that is receding, if not into the past, at any rate into the background. In the cities and big towns a new industrialized life is growing up that will have to develop its own standards of conduct, and in which some of the older virtues and vices will doubtless be lost. But even here the new ideas will have to be grafted on to the accumulated past, and for a proper understanding of the Persia of to-day, we must have an insight into the Persia out of which it is growing.

Our proverbs show us a people living close to the earth. There is much accurate observation of nature—of the weather, the seasons, wild life. It is, however, a settled village life that we see rather than the nomadic life of the tribes. Tribal lore seems to have contributed little to Persian proverbial wisdom, though doubtless its absence is due to the isolation and inaccessibility of the tribes rather than their failure to crystallize their experience into proverbial form. But the proverbs we have are those of people living in houses ; they deal with household furniture and utensils, with household occupations, cleaning, sleeping, cooking, sewing. There is much of family and domestic life—relations with husbands and wives, neighbours, shopkeepers, the public baths, births, deaths and marriages, and so on. Among the occupations referred to we find shepherds, camel-drivers, farmers, woodcutters, charcoal-burners, potters, carpenters, millers, dyers, tailors, washermen and barbers. The busy life of the bazaar is revealed, with its haggling traders, crafty merchants and business transactions. The personalities of community life are met, the village headman, the *molla*, the *qazi*, the teacher and the doctor ; their world is organized, there is law, authority, religion. With the outside world indeed there is little contact. Travel is looked on with distaste, the sea with horror. Kings and princes, or the heroes and heroines of literature, figure from time to time, but in a rather remote way. It is the common man, the peasant or villager, who is the central figure, and it is his problems that are observed.

He finds himself in an insecure and chancy world, in which a man must have patience and a sense of humour if he is to survive. He is urged to be cautious but persevering, self-reliant and honest. Generosity, hospitality, gratitude and wisdom are the virtues encouraged, trickery, greed, miserliness, injustice, vanity and selfishness the vices, evidently all too common, to be deplored. The ideal man of the proverbs has the qualities of the Zoroastrian hero—pure speech, pure vision, pure deeds—tempered by the practical wisdom that stems from centuries of hardship and disaster.

Proverbs are still widely used by Persians of all classes. Persian speech as a whole is full of picturesque phrases and expressive idioms, of which the following may serve as a small sample : " My tongue grew hairs " (I was tired out with talking, giving advice) ; " Don't boil, your milk will go dry " (said to someone getting unreasonably angry) ; of a great uproar, " A dog couldn't have recognized his master," " If you had dropped a needle, it wouldn't have reached the floor." To someone who apologizes for turning his back on you you may reply, " A flower has neither back nor front " ; of an aged man it might be said that " when they erected the arch of the sky, he put up half of it ". And many would sympathize with the comment on someone's illegible handwriting : " If you put it in the sun, it would walk."

It is unfortunately impossible to render in translation the conciseness with which many of these sayings and proverbs are expressed, still less to give any idea of their rhythm and rhyme. Something of this may perhaps be sensed from the following examples, in the original language, of some of the proverbs quoted later in this book.

Fel'fel ma'bin ché 'rizé, besh'kan be'bin ché 'tizé.

Don't judge a pepper-corn by its smallness, crack it and see how sharp it is. (Page 29.)

Cha'hâr di'vâri ekhti'yâri.

Four walls make a free man. (Page 38.)

'Har ké 'fekr-e 'khishast, 'kusé be-'fekr-e 'rishast.

Everybody thinks of himself ; even the thin-beard thinks of his beard. (Page 41.)

Na'khod khor'i na'kas de'hi, 'gandé ko'ni be'sag de'hi.

You don't eat it yourself nor give it to others ; you let it go rotten and then give it to the dog. (Page 49.)

'Kur-e bi'nâ behtar az bi'nâ-e 'kur.

A blind man who sees is better than a seeing man who is blind. (Page 57.)

Ta'lâ ké ' pâk ast, ché hâ'jatash be'khâk ast ?

Gold in its purity need fear nothing from the earth. (Page 89.)

The simplicity and directness of these examples is evidence of their colloquial origin. Most of the proverbs quoted in this book are in fact colloquial; whether or not this form is the oldest (and there is no doubt that a few have a literary origin), it is certainly the most effective. Many have been versified or given literary form by one writer or another; but even the most brilliant poets have only succeeded in blurring the vividness of the original.

In making the present selection the writer has had in mind the thought that a good proverb should have a certain pungency, a modicum of wit. There are in Persian, as in all languages, a great many platitudinous sayings—"Mankind are members one of another," "True piety consists in serving the people," "Obedience is the root of prosperity," "Do not put off to-day's work till to-morrow," "Silence indicates consent," "Contentment makes a man rich," "He who has gold has power," "Envy is a disease for which there is no cure." Since many of these ideas have been more wittily expressed in proverbial form, it has been thought proper to omit them in their natural state, even though they are in common usage.

Selection has in any case had to be drastic. One of the largest modern collections, that by Ali Akbar Dehkhoda, contains some 25,000 proverbs, and even that list is by no means complete. Persian proverbs are part of the stream of popular lore and legend that appears to have begun in India or Central Asia and passed by degrees through the Middle East to Europe. It is indeed impossible to draw a hard and fast line, other than that of language, between the national folk-lores of this vast area. Equivalents, often word for word the same, are found in Urdu, Persian, Armenian, Kurdish, Arabic, Turkish, and coming further west, in Greek, Latin and the modern European languages. In East and West alike people "bury the hatchet", they " lay the axe to the root ", they ask " who will bell the cat ", they observe that " dog does not eat dog ", and they laugh at " the pot for calling the kettle black ". The national differences lie rather in mode of expression or perhaps choice of imagery, though naturally every community has its own private sayings based on local legend.

Such, for example, is the exclamation employed, especially in Isfahan, to express astonishment or wonder: " We have journeyed through three hundred and sixty-six valleys, but we have never yet seen a man with two heads ! " The " three hundred and sixty-six valleys " are supposed to refer to a desolate waste, some say near Isfahan, others on the way to Mazandaran, which, the story goes, was once haunted by a demon with the habit of licking the feet of travellers while they slept and sucking their blood. One night two travellers, an Isfahani and a Turk, found themselves stranded in this ill-omened place. For a while they kept themselves awake by telling stories, but eventually they could keep it up no longer. Isfahanis, however, are noted for their ingenuity and resourcefulness, and this one was no exception. " I'm a demon myself ! " he exclaimed. " Where's the demon that can touch me ? Now, let us lie down in opposite directions, you put your feet under my armpits, and I'll put mine under yours, and then we'll be quite safe." Sure enough, before long the demon smelt human flesh, and sniffing round the sleeping men, he found a head at one end and a head at the other. At a loss, he " bit the finger of amazement and disappointment " and exclaimed, " By God ! I have journeyed through three hundred and sixty-six valleys, but I have never yet seen a man with two heads ! "

As will be seen, many of the proverbs quoted in this book are associated with fables of this kind. There is no telling whether the stories are the origin of the proverbs or the proverbs of the stories, and it is indeed quite unprofitable to speculate. It is certainly true that it is easier to identify the proverbs themselves than it is to track down the legends that go with them. One assiduous worker in this field, Amir Qoli Amini, gives the following account of his difficulties.

"I had to spend a great deal of my time in company and conversation with ordinary, illiterate people, and, as they put it, 'to give a heart and take a kidney',[1] before I could profit from their invaluable store of information. But after a time I found that the conversation of a corn-chandler, a grocer or a ploughman, even though he could not distinguish a pronoun from a preposition, left a stimulating and indeed disturbing impression on me that I would never have got from conversation with an educated man.

"Often when I asked them questions about proverbs and fables, I would get such a generous response, they would so lavish on me the wealth of lore stored in their memories, that I was moved to an extent that I could never have imagined. The more ample and delightful their stories were, the more my interest and enthusiasm was aroused. When a goldsmith told me a particular story, I felt as though he had freely given me the finest masterpieces of the skilled craft of his two hands, with all its gold and jewellery.

"I was not content with craftsmen, but associated as freely as I could with servants, cab-drivers and taxi-drivers, and in the same way, when I went into the villages, I lived with the peasants. Whenever the opportunity offered itself, I at once took out of my pocket my notebook or some scraps of paper, and began asking questions.

"'Now, my friend, what do you know about our proverbs? Tell, me, what is the original story of the proverb "An apple thrown into the air will turn a thousand times before it reaches the ground," or "Escape may lie between this pillar and that"?'

"Out of every hundred people it usually happened that ninety-nine claimed ignorance. Fifty per cent could only answer my questions with a few simple and hackneyed sayings.

[1] To converse with warmth and enthusiasm.

"Is it not surprising that a craftsman or a peasant may know hundreds of proverbs, and yet, unless the appropriate moment arises and one of them comes automatically and instinctively to his tongue, he cannot call to mind half a dozen from the treasury of his subconscious in order to repeat them to you?"

One does not always meet the difficulties that Mr. Amini encountered. There are still many—from professional story-tellers to nurses and grandmothers—who have a wealth of such fables and legends at the tip of the tongue, and are only too willing to retail them to anyone patient enough to listen. It is unfortunately true that little enough has been done to commit all this material to writing. Those who hold it are mostly illiterate, and receive and pass it on by word of mouth. Some stories of course have found their way into collections like the *Thousand and One Nights*; another very famous collection is that known in India as the *Fables of Bidpai*, and in Persia and the Middle East as the *Book of Kalilé and Demné*. Proverbs and traditional stories are also constantly used by Persian poets and other writers. Sa'di's *Golestan* (Rose-garden) and *Bustan* (Flower-garden), anthologies of the wisdom and fable accumulated by him during his extensive travels, have themselves given currency to sayings and aphorisms whose originals must date from long before the thirteenth century in which he wrote. The same is true of the *Masnavi* or mystical poem of Jalal ad-Din Rumi, sometimes described as the Persian Koran, and of the works of poets like Jami, Nezami, Attar and Hafez. The Koran itself and the many Traditions of the Prophet, authentic and otherwise, are a further source of present-day popular lore.

Some idea of the antiquity of these fables may be gathered from the fact that many of them are to be found among those attributed to Aesop. Readers of the present work will recognize "The Old Man and Death" (No. CXXII in Thomas

James's version, page 12 in the present book), "The Dog and the Shadow" (No. XXIV and page 26), "The Boasting Traveller" (No. CXCV and page 59), "The Fox and the Crow" (No. CLXXXIII and page 67), "The Ant and the Grasshopper" (No. XII and page 70), and "The Thief and his Mother" (No. CI and page 73); there is also a similarity in theme between the stories on pages 37 and 53, and "The Stag in the Oxstall" (No. LIII) and "The Miser" (No. CXCII). More thorough inquiry would no doubt reveal further similarities, and indeed there is a profitable field of research in a detailed comparison and correlation of the folk-lore of India, the Middle East and Europe.

So much for the similarities, the common basis of the proverbial wisdom of the Old World. If there were no more to it than that there might seem to be little justification for the study of its manifestations in any particular community. But in fact, of course, there is a great deal more. There may be a common stream of ideas, but as they pass through each cultural area they become changed and transmuted through contact with and absorption by local character, tradition and custom. Of no people is this more true than of the Persians, whose capacity for incorporating and "Persianizing" foreign importations in all fields of thought has become a byword. A study of their proverbs and the folk-lore attached to them will not only give us an idea of the outside influences to which they have been subjected in the past, but will also illuminate their ways of thought and their national characteristics to an extent that perhaps no other medium can do. The literary classics of the past and the present will give us the products of the best minds of Persia in poetry, science, history and philosophy; but these great minds emerged from a common heritage that has a formative effect on all those who share it. Only through folk-lore can the outsider hope to gain even a glimpse of this heritage ; yet without a knowledge of it he cannot begin to understand why Persians—or for the matter of that, Arabs, Frenchmen or Russians—think and behave as they do.

It is no easy task. Even when all the relevant material has been collected (and, as we have seen, that process is by no means complete), we have still the practical problem of idiomatic translation from a language structurally different from ours. More significant still, it is a language whose background is entirely different from that of our own. Even the scenery, the climate, the wild life—the sources, in fact, from which the images are drawn—are all different ; a loaf of bread means one thing to us, another thing to a Persian. Nor are ideas and images associated in the same way ; in Persia, for instance, the sun is generally a torment from which one is glad to escape, in Britain it is a rare and welcome visitor. The problem becomes progressively more complex as we move into the sphere of abstract ideas. We are up against a whole new way of thought, a whole new culture, and we can only absorb it gradually and by contact and study over a long period of time, just as a child gradually absorbs the culture and ways of thought of his parents.

The present book has no such ambition. It does not even set out to give a comprehensive or representative survey of the proverbs of Persia, but rather to take a few at random, a handful, as they themselves would say, from the donkey-load. Many of them the writer first encountered in conversation and discussion in Persia, though the majority are also to be found in one or other of the Persian publications listed in the first part of the bibliography. There are, however, a number that do not seem yet to have made their way into print and, moreover, these Persian publications are not easily accessible even to scholars. The writer would prefer to think of the present book not so much as a fresh contribution to the knowledge of Persian proverbs, as a means of bringing them before the English-speaking public for the first time. In defence of its shortcomings of purpose and of achievement, the writer can only claim that " a house is built to the ability of its builder ", or, as the Arabs say, " the gift is the measure of the giver ".

One final point needs to be made in connexion with the system used for the spelling of Persian names and words. There is unfortunately as yet no accepted system of transliteration for Persian, as there is for Arabic ; the latter, though commonly used for Persian, is quite unsuitable to it and in no way represents the current pronunciation of the Persian language. The system adopted in the present book is based on that devised by the writer for his *Colloquial Persian* in 1941. It may be helpful to mention that the accent in Persian generally falls on the last syllable. The only deviations from the " system " are names and words that have become anglicized to an extent that precludes experiment. Thus one would not wish to interfere with bazaar, Koran, Avicenna, dervish, kabob, Kabul or Turcoman ; and for the same reason words like Isfahan, Kurd, Sunnite, Muhammad, Fatima, Kerbela, Azerbaijan and Turkestan have been left in their common form.

1. THE FLEETING WORLD

The proverbs that follow have for convenience been divided, somewhat arbitrarily, into various groups according to the general topics with which they deal. It goes without saying that no such division exists in the minds of those who use them, and it may even be misleading in that it brings into too great prominence the apparent contradictions always inherent in proverbial lore. In this first section we are concerned with the vagaries of fate and the changing fortunes of life on earth. Sudden disaster and utter destitution have been all too common features of life in Persia. Of a poor man it might be said that "he has not a sigh to trade for a groan", or that "his pocket is cleaner than a molla's gaberdine". "Even death", for such a man, "is a wedding"; "the water of his life has been poured into a muslin sieve". Death itself is a common theme. "His life is like the sun sinking over the mountain"; "his chin has taken on the smell of the Merciful One". And there is a macabre note of humour in the comment on a man long dead: "He has worn out seven shrouds." In the face of this pessimism it is hardly surprising that many proverbs urge patience, submission to fate, acceptance of things as they are, making the best of circumstances—and even an optimistic belief that good will come out of bad, that every man's life is guided by a lucky star.

In the ant's house the dew is a flood.

A slight loss is a great one to a poor man.

Let the thief who strikes at the end of the night strike at its beginning.

If bad fortune is in store for us, then let it come at once.

One hump on top of another.

The story goes that one night a hunchback went into a public bath, and found a fairy wedding in progress. He at once joined the festivities, and so entertained the company by his comic antics that they took his hump away from him, and placed it on a shelf. This story spread round the town the following day, and another hunchback decided to profit by his friend's experience. Unfortunately he omitted to notice that the gathering of fairies on this occasion was for the purpose of mourning, and the latter were so incensed at his unseemly behaviour that, instead of taking his hump away, they fastened the other one on top of it. The phrase is now used of anyone who, whether through his own fault or not, finds yet another difficulty added to his former ones.

He sheltered from the rain under the drain-pipe.

He got out of the well and fell into the pit.

He escaped from the thief's clutches, and was caught by the fortune-teller.

Three of many proverbs comparable to our own "He fell out of the frying pan into the fire."

You haven't the power to give me a donkey, but you're quite clever enough to kill me.

According to a Bakhtiyari tale, a woodcutter was plodding along with a heavy load on his back. At length he dropped it on the ground, and, throwing himself wearily down, began to bewail his fate. "O God," he cried, "either send me a donkey or send me death!" Just at that moment a huge boulder came rolling down the mountain-side and landed a few feet from him. "So!" he exclaimed in fear and anger, "You haven't the power to give me a donkey, but you're quite clever enough to kill me!" A similar story is to be found in Aesop and Lafontaine. The proverb, like the following one, is used by Persians when someone has hoped for good and receives harm.

Of all the prophets you would *choose Jerjis.*

Jerjis is the Oriental counterpart to the Christian St. George. One day a mouse was caught by a cat, and finding itself held tightly between the creature's teeth, bethought himself of a trick. " O most noble cat," he cried, " O lion of courage and bravery, I am fearful for your fate in the next world if you shed my blood unlawfully. I urge you therefore, before you swallow me, to pronounce the name of one of the prophets, so that you may be absolved of all guilt." The cat, however, was a wily one, and saw through the mouse's plan ; if he were to open his mouth to speak, the mouse would escape. But by pronouncing the name "Jerjis", he was able not only to keep his teeth clenched, but to thrust them right through the mouse's body. Hence the latter's woeful exclamation.

Stones rain upon a broken door.

Wherever there is a stone, a lame foot will find it.

It's the lame foot that has the tight shoe.

In other words, " It never rains but it pours."

No colour is deeper than black.

Things couldn't be any worse.

When water covers the head, a hundred fathoms are as one.

That is to say, " As well be hung for a sheep as a lamb." Compare the following :

The drowning man is not troubled by rain.

This proverb is found in Arabic, Turkish and Armenian as well as Persian, and is used by Sa'di in several places.

A stick has two ends.

Every affair may turn out well or badly.

If fortune turns against you, even the horse in the stable becomes a donkey.

If fortune turns against you, even jelly breaks your tooth.

Even a melon-seed may come between husband and wife.

A minor incident may change the course of destiny.

Even the handsome Ahmad caught small-pox.

No one is safe from the changes and chances of fate.

The arrow that has left the bow never returns.

Words once spoken cannot be recalled.

He who puffs at the lamp of God will singe his beard.

It is no use striving against the decrees of God. This proverb is based on a passage in the Koran (lxi. 8), and is also found in the *Masnavi* of Jalal ad-Din Rumi and the mystical poetry of Sana'i.

God drives the vessel where he will, no matter how the captain rants.

A verse from the *Golestan* of Sa'di.

Death is a camel that lies down at every door.

When its time has arrived, the prey comes to the hunter.

A verse from Jami, to be compared with the following verse from Naser-e Khosrou: "When the camel is about to die, it comes to the edge of the well."

Jump once, little locust, jump twice, but the third time you'll be caught.

Don't tempt providence too often. This proverb occurs in the middle of a rather lengthy story concerning a carpenter who, through a lucky guess, discovered the princess's lost ring and found himself appointed as the king's fortune-teller. He bluffed his way successfully through the next problem that he had to solve, and then one day he had to accompany the king on a hunting expedition. On the way a locust hopped on to the king's saddle ; he flicked it away, but it jumped back again. The same thing happened again, and the third time the king grabbed it in his hand, and keeping his fist clenched sent for the fortune-teller, who was at the back of the cavalcade. "What have I got in my hand?" he asked. The fortune-teller, terrified out of his wits, could only think of his two previous lucky escapes, and cried out, "Jump once, little locust, jump twice, but the third time you'll be caught." The king was amazed at his powers, and lavished rewards upon him. Nevertheless the experience was too much for the humble carpenter, who found some pretext to leave the court, and escaped to a distant land, never to return.

Death comes once and sorrow but once.

Said to someone who continues to lament over past disasters, even when the excuse for it is past.

Patience is the key to all things.

In Arabic there is a similar proverb: "Patience is the key to consolation."

Patience is bitter, but its fruit is sweet.

This proverb is used several times by Sa'di.

Let the world after death be ocean or rill.

Let the world after death be a mosque or a synagogue.

It will all be the same in a hundred years.

Grief only brings more loss to your purse.

It's no use crying over spilt milk.

Let us think of to-morrow when to-morrow comes.

Don't meet troubles half-way. This is the first half of a verse from Nezami, which continues: "It is far better to enjoy ourselves to-night."

Woman is a torment, but, O God, let no home be without torment!

Woman is a torment, but she is worth buying with your life.

Blessings on the first grave-robber!

Better the devil you know than the devil you don't know. In a certain city a thief made a practice of stealing the winding-sheets from the graves of the newly-buried dead. The outraged populace complained to the governor, who after lengthy investigations caught the thief and consigned him to prison. But he was succeeded by another thief who not only stole the shrouds but treated the bodies in an irreverent and scurrilous manner. Hence the people's cry from the heart, which has become proverbial.

I'll eat what I've paid for, however much it croaks.

A Lori tribesman came to town one day, and seeing some tempting vegetables in a shop, bought some together with some flaps of bread and, squatting down by the door of the mosque, began to eat them. It so happened that there was a frog concealed among the leaves, but the Lor, supposing it to be some new kind of vegetable, folded it into his bread and, in spite of its protests, proceeded to swallow it. The proverb is used by Isfahani merchants when they have made a bad bargain, but insist on making the best of it.

If you've no mother, get on with your stepmother.

Make the best of things as they are.

If you haven't a house to fit an elephant, don't make friends with the mahout.

This verse is from Sa'di, who has another on the same theme: "Either be content with your troubles, or throw your entrails to the crows," that is to say, by trying to escape from your present troubles, you may expose yourself to something worse.

No lamp burns till morning.

Nothing lasts for ever, perfect happiness is impossible.

Behind every smile lie two hundred tears.

The meaning is similar to the last, but it is interesting to note the reversed form of it quoted below (page 18).

He most values safety who experiences danger.

The story of this proverb occurs in the *Golestan* of Sa'di, and relates how a king, while on a sea-voyage, noticed a Persian slave who, never having been at sea before, was making a great commotion and refusing to be reassured. A wise man on the ship offered to cure him, and succeeded in doing so by throwing him into the sea and allowing him to sink beneath the water several times before dragging him out by the hair. After this experience the slave gave no more trouble.

Gruel is better than nothing.

Half a loaf is better than no bread.

Even loss can be a profit.

Many popular tales centre round the character of Molla Nasr ad-Din, who may be said to represent the rustic combination of stupidity and simple logic. One of his practices, it is said, was to buy eggs at nine for a penny and sell them at ten for a penny. When asked why he did this, he replied, "Even loss can be a profit," meaning that at least people would know that he was in business. The proverb is used to console someone who has suffered a heavy loss.

The blind want only eyes.

People say this to a man when they at last give him something for which he has been asking.

Hope is born of despair.

Every tear has a smile behind it.

Rumi caps this with the line : " He who sees through to the end is the happiest of mortals."

Whatever happens is good.

It's all for the best. " The gifts of God are good." (Arabic.)

Some heads have little sustenance, but there are none without any.

There's always bread for an open mouth.

A molla was expatiating from the pulpit on the delights of paradise, and was describing in some detail the charms of the countless *huris* who would greet and minister to the faithful on their arrival. At length a voice came from among the women, " And what about us ? " The molla looked in their direction and replied, " Don't worry. There's always bread for an open mouth." Said in order to comfort those who complain of their hard lot.

Man lives on hope.

A broken hand works, but not a broken heart.

Don't give way to despair.

An apple thrown into the air will turn a thousand times before it reaches the ground.

It was related of Chengiz Khan that, whenever he went out hunting, he had a hundred prisoners beheaded before the gates of the city, no doubt with the idea of propitiating the gods and securing a good day's sport. On one occasion the prisoners were headed by a wise old man who, when the sword was about to fall, dodged to one side and threw himself on the ground. Chengiz said angrily, " You foolish old man, how can you expect to escape, loaded down with chains as you are? Why don't you accept your fate at once, instead of trying to dodge?" " They say," answered the old man calmly, " that an apple thrown into the air will turn a thousand times before it reaches the ground. How am I to know that in that short space of time something might not happen to save me from death?" Chengiz angrily took a large ruby, the size of an apple, from his pocket and threw it into the air, saying, " Do you really think that something can happen before this ruby reaches the ground?" Hardly were the words out of his mouth when the heavy ruby struck his horse's head, the horse reared, and Chengiz was thrown heavily to the ground and killed. His retinue, in terror of their lives now that their master was gone, took to their heels, and the prisoners returned in triumph to the city.

Escape may lie between this pillar and that.

An innocent man was condemned to death by an unjust governor, and when the executioner had bound him to a pillar and was about to cut off his head, the victim begged that he might be bound to the next pillar instead. The executioner laughed at him, saying, " What can you hope to gain from so brief an interval? You might just as well let me finish my job." But eventually he gave way to the man's entreaties; and while he was engaged in untying him and fastening him to the next pillar, the king chanced to pass by and asked the meaning of the large crowd that had gathered. On being told, he sent for the condemned man, who was able to convince him of his innocence, and so escaped death.

God gives pain, and also gives the cure.

There is a cure for every ill.

May God always bless us with such evil!

A pious man bought a cow in the market and set out for his home. He was followed by a thief who planned to steal his cow. On the way the thief fell in with another man who revealed himself as a demon who planned to take the pious man's life. As they drew near to the latter's house, where the cow was now tied up, it occurred to the thief that if the demon killed the pious man first, his family might be aroused, and it would be impossible to steal the cow. At the same time the demon thought that, if the thief stole the cow first, the pious man would be awakened by its bellowing, and so would escape death. Each began to ask the other to wait and take second place, and eventually they came to blows. The thief began to shout, "O pious man, here is a demon who has come to take your life!" while the demon shouted back, "O pious man, here is a thief who has come to steal your cow!" In the end the man and his family were aroused, the thief and the demon took to their heels, and the pious man drew the above moral for the benefit of his family.

He who has a lucky star sleeps on his back.

A lucky man may do as he likes.

2. PRACTICAL WISDOM

Many Persian proverbs urge one to have a sense of proportion, not to take things too seriously. " Don't make a rope of a hair," we are told; after all, " Heaven will not get a hole in it ". Be practical; " two half donkey-loads make no more than a whole one ", in other words, it is six of one and half a dozen of the other. Don't go to extremes, " don't be as salty as that, or as tasteless as this ". The good business man is admired; indeed, " the merchant is the friend of God ". There is no discredit in looking after your own interests first, and the cleverer you are the better you will do this. There is a lot to be said for the sharp fellow who is like " water under straw ", who has " a cat under his arm "; it is hardly surprising that the man who has " thrown out the cat from under his arm " has not so much decided to abandon deceitful ways, as let the cat out of the bag. The emphasis of all the proverbs in this section is on caution, expediency and worldliness.

When a hundred comes, ninety is here as well.

The whole includes the parts. The Arabs have a saying, " When the sun rises, there is no need of the moon."

An elephant alive costs a hundred tumans, *but so does a dead one.*

Don't complain of minor faults in something.

Stretch your foot to the length of your blanket.

In other words, cut your coat according to your cloth. This proverb is very popular in both Persian and Arabic literature, and has been used by many of the great poets, including Hafez, Attar, Naser-e Khosrou and Asadi.

Eat little, sleep sound.

Waste not, want not.

An ear of corn has only one head.

Don't expect too much.

Don't take a bite too big for your mouth.

Don't bite off more than you can chew.

You can only get meat from the side of a cow.

You must only expect something from the man who has the power to do it.

Carpentry is no trade for a monkey.

Threshing corn is no task for a goat.

It's the bird with the hooked beak that eats millet.

These three are all similar to our " Let the cobbler stick to his last." The second is a verse from Sa'di and continues, " It requires an ox and a hardened man." The story of the first is to be found in the *Anvar-e Soheili*, a later version of the *Kalilé va Demné* referred to in the Introduction, and runs as follows : A monkey was watching a carpenter at work, and noticed that, as he sawed through the length of a log of wood, he would put wedges one after the other into the crack in order to hold the sides apart and make room for the saw. When the carpenter had gone, the monkey slipped into his place, and proceeded to take out the wedge that was in place without inserting another further down the crack. The two halves of the timber sprang together and caught the monkey's tail. In pain and despair he cried out, " I should have stuck to my own task of picking fruit," but there was no escape, and when the carpenter returned later he caught and killed him.

Don't sleep in a troubled place, and you won't dream a troubled dream.

Beware of a rickety wall, a savage dog, and a quarrelsome woman.

The first condition of safety is caution.

Walls have mice and mice have ears.

The Arabs have a saying, " If you talk by night, lower your voice, and if you talk by day, keep your eyes open."

Don't jump into the water where there is no ford.

Don't cut without measuring.

Look before you leap. A Kurdish proverb says, " First see the mother, and then ask for her daughter's hand."

Hearing is never as good as seeing.

From truth to falsehood is no more than four fingers.

Four fingers, that is to say, the distance between eye and ear. The meaning is, of course, the same as the preceding.

He who has been bitten by a snake fears a piece of string.

A burnt child dreads the fire.

Use your enemy's hand to catch a snake.

To avoid disfavour, follow the crowd.

When in Rome, do as Rome does. The story goes that the whole population of a certain city were suddenly afflicted with madness, with the exception of one man who had been absent at the time. On his return he found the whole place in confusion, with the people running around naked, laughing, dancing, fighting, climbing trees, and so on. Dumb with amazement, he sat down in a corner, when suddenly he was observed by one of the citizens who, seeing him clothed and silent, cried out to the others, " Look ! Look ! A madman ! " The whole crowd seized upon the unfortunate man and began to hurl him to and fro, shouting " A madman ! A madman ! " In despair, he tore off his clothes and began to join in the shouting, whereupon the crowd, seeing that he had regained his sanity, left him alone once more.

A stone thrown at the right time is better than gold given at the wrong time.

A tear in place is better than a smile out of place.

Stone breaks stone.

Iron smooths iron.

Iron takes iron from the furnace.

All have the meaning of " diamond cuts diamond " ; it may take harsh measures to achieve a desirable result. Similarly the proverb that follows.

It takes a needle to get a thorn from one's foot.

He has eaten so many snakes that he has become a viper.

A man who has wide experience in crime will quickly recognize crime in others ; he will be a thief to catch a thief.

He is partner to the thief and escort to the caravan.

He is running with the hare and hunting with the hounds.

Take care to burn neither spit nor kabobs.

Keep on good terms with both sides.

Don't give thanks for your catch till you've eaten it.

It is said that foxes have a habit of shamming dead in order to deceive and trap other birds and animals. A wily crow once saw a fox doing this, but in order to make sure that he was really dead, he drew a line round the body and went away saying to himself, "If the fox is still inside the line to-morrow, I will know that he is really dead." As soon as he had gone, the fox got up, but early next morning he returned and lay down as before inside the line. The crow, seeing him still there, came up in all confidence, but before he could peck out the fox's eyes, he was seized. Seeing no chance of escape, he said to the fox, "I have no objection to your eating me, but you should at least say grace first." The fox opened his mouth to give thanks to God, and the crow flew off. Notice the similarity and contrast between this story and the one on page 12.

Don't sell the bearskin before you've caught the bear.

Two friends went out bear-hunting. For four days they saw nothing, and each night they slept in a nearby village, pledging the bear's skin against the cost of their lodging. On the fifth day a huge bear appeared, and Ali said nervously to his friend, "I don't mind confessing that I'm afraid to take on this bear." Hasan laughed and retorted, "I've always known that you were incapable of taking on a cock, let alone a bear. Just you leave him to me." So Ali scrambled like lightning up the nearest tree, and Hasan stood with his gun at the ready. The bear came lumbering on, and Hasan began to grow more and more scared. At length he raised his gun to his shoulder, but by now he was trembling so much that, before he could take proper aim, his gun went off and missed the target. Hasan, remembering that bears never touch a dead body, threw himself flat and held his breath. The bear came up, snuffed all round him and finally made off. Ali, who had been watching the whole affair from his tree, now came down and, congratulating Hasan on his escape, asked him, "What did the bear whisper in your ear?"

"Oh," replied Hasan, "he told me never to sell the bear's skin before I'd caught the bear."

Aesop has a similar story with a different moral.

A thief is a king till he's caught.

They count the chickens in autumn.

Wait and see how things turn out. By autumn many of the spring chickens will have been lost.

Don't lose your head like the dog in the story.

A dog stole a piece of meat from a butcher's shop and ran off. In order to escape the butcher, he jumped into a river and began to swim across. In mid-river he suddenly caught sight of his own reflection, and supposing it to be another dog with a piece of meat, opened his mouth to grab this new prize. The meat fell from his jaws and was carried away by the stream. Thus the proverb advises one not to give up the substance for the shadow.

He lost a camel and went after its saddle.

He worries about trifles and ignores fundamentals.

All's not a walnut that's round.

Not every bearded man's your father.

All is not gold that glitters.

A single rose does not mean spring.

Persians also use the expression, "One swallow does not make a summer."

Trust in God, but tie your camel.

One day the Prophet's camel was lost, and only recovered after a long search. The Prophet asked his groom, "Why didn't you tie back the camel's knee [1] when you left it to rest?" "I didn't tie it

[1] Camels in the desert are normally fastened in this way.

because I put my trust in God," answered the groom. "Both tie and trust," replied the Prophet. Originally an Arabic proverb and story, the Persian form is taken from the *Masnavi* of Jalal ad-Din Rumi.

Necessity turns lion into fox.

Necessity turns even the noblest men into deceivers. This also is a verse from Rumi's *Masnavi*.

The lamp in the home is not for the mosque.

Charity begins at home.

A fruit that hangs out of the garden will be stoned by every passer-by.

Don't expose your family and property to the depredations of others.

Look after your money and don't make your neighbour a thief.

Don't put temptation in the way of others.

An account is an account and a brother a brother.

Never mind about brotherhood, goats are 700 dinars *apiece.*

Where business is concerned, personal relations must not enter. The Arabs say, "Live together like brothers and do business like strangers."

They tie up an ass where his master wishes.

He who rents his room lives as he pleases.

He who pays the piper calls the tune.

Gold brings gold, lack of gold a headache.

Oil adds to oil, but groats remain dry.

A slap in hand is better than a gift to come.

A bird in the hand is worth two in the bush. So also :

Vinegar in hand is better than halva *to come.*

The drum-corps camel is not frightened by the noise.

Nader's drum was fastened on his back.

Both these proverbs imply that the man will not be frightened by someone's empty threats, for he has heard plenty of them before. According to the first story, a child was left to guard a field of corn, and had before him a drum which he beat repeatedly in order to scare away birds and other beasts. It so happened that one of the camels of Soltan Mahmud's drum corps had strayed, and wandered into the field in search of fodder. The child beat his drum with all his might, but the camel would not go ; and a passer-by remarked, " You are ' beating cold iron ', you are wasting your time, for he is a drum-corps camel, and his eyes and ears are full of such sounds." In the second story, a camel which had formerly carried the drum of the conqueror Nader Shah lost its way and wandered into the yard of an old widow. The widow tried to frighten him away by beating on a large brass tray, but the camel said, " We are not afraid, we have seen plenty of this sort of thing, for once Nader's drum was fastened to our back."

Rain will not come at the prayer of a black cat.

We came at no one's bidding, and we go at no one's curse.

Both these expressions may be used as a retort to someone who abuses you, implying that his words will have no effect.

You don't feed a donkey sugar and greens.

Why cast pearls before swine? Compare :

Why play music for a deaf man, or dance for a blind man?

Sweep clean the house of your friends, but don't knock at the door of your foe.

The following story comes from the *Golestan* of Sa'di. A poor man stole a rug from the house of his friend. The governor ordered his hand to be cut off,[1] but his friend interceded for him, saying "I have forgiven him." Replied the governor, "I cannot stretch the limits of the law for the sake of your intercession." "You are right," replied the friend, "but no one who steals *vaqf* (religious) property is liable to have his hand cut off, and since the poor own nothing, anything that they have is a *vaqf* for those who need it." The governor revoked the thief's punishment and rebuked him, saying, "What possessed you to steal from the house of a sincere friend like this?" "Your Honour," replied the thief, "have you not heard that one may sweep clean the house of a friend, but shouldn't even knock at the door of a foe?"

A sponsor will be caught by the purse or caught by the collar.

It is not worth while to go surety for anyone.

If you die for someone, see that he has a fever for you.

Have some practical purpose in putting yourself out for anyone.

Show him death, and he'll be content with fever.

If you propose harsh conditions to someone, he will gladly agree to what you really want.

Don't judge a pepper-corn by its smallness, crack it and see how sharp it is.

An insignificant-looking man may have sharp wits.

[1] The traditional punishment for theft.

He extends as far beneath the earth as he does above.

This comment is also applied to a small but clever man.

It is better for an ant to have wings.

The Arabic version runs, " If God had wanted to destroy the ant, he would have given it wings." In other words, it is better for a sly fellow to keep to his own methods, and not to imitate those greater or more powerful than himself.

3. FORESIGHT AND SELF-RELIANCE

Several proverbs in the previous section urged self-reliance and independence, and in this section the theme is continued. He who wishes to "mount his donkey", "to take it across the bridge", in other words, to put his affairs in order and achieve his aim, must have foresight and must be prepared to expend effort and suffer pain. If he does this, he will undoubtedly "pull his blanket out of the water"; he may even "hit two targets with one arrow", or if you prefer it, "eat both from the nosebag and from the manger". In general, we are on more familiar ground here. There is less of sly cunning, more of honest endeavour; though as yet we do not find very much in the way of an ideal set up before us. That, perhaps, is to come; in the meantime, it is enough that we should stand on our own feet.

The spring may be dammed with a rod.

This is the first half of a well-known verse from the *Golestan*. It continues, "Let it swell to full size and you may not cross it with an elephant." In other words, a stitch in time saves nine.

War at the beginning is better than peace at the end.

An ounce of prevention is worth a pound of cure.

Make bread while the oven is hot.

After Sohrab's death the antidote.

This proverb comes from the well-known story of Rostam and Sohrab, as given in the *Shahnamé* of Ferdousi. It will be remembered that Rostam unknowingly fought a duel with his son Sohrab, of whose existence he had not previously even been aware, and who was now the champion of Turan, the enemy of Iran. Sohrab was mortally wounded, and revealed the secret of his parenthood to his father. Rostam, distraught, pleaded with his sovereign Kei Kavus to let him have an infallible antidote from the royal treasury. The king at first refused, and when he finally agreed, it was too late. Both this and the proverb that follows have the meaning of " After death the doctor," or " Don't shut the stable door after the horse has gone." Compare :

An antidote from distant Iraq will not cure a deadly snakebite.

If you have no door, why have a doorman ?

He whose wife dies sighs for a sister-in-law.

Said of someone who loses something that he did not value highly enough.

First dig a well and then steal a minaret.

Plan your task before you start it. The story goes that the people of a village near Sabzevar plotted to steal a particular minaret, and for this purpose took a hundred donkeys and lined them up in front of the minaret, and prepared to lower it on to their backs. At this juncture an old man asked them, " Have you dug a well in which to hide it ? " The two proverbs that follow are variations on this theme.

First see the headman and then fleece the village.

First build your cowshed and then buy a cow for it.

Others planted for us to eat ; now we plant for others to eat.

Anushirvan the Just, when riding through the country-side, saw an old man of eighty busily employed in planting walnut saplings. " Old man," he said, " you know that it will be years before those saplings bear fruit. Why do you waste so much effort on something that you can never share ? " " Sire," replied the old man, " others planted for us to eat, now we plant for others to eat." The king was pleased with this answer and gave the old man a hundred *ashrafis*. " Sire," said the old man, " others planted for us to eat ; we too planted for others to eat, but we did not die, and so we ourselves ate." The king was even more pleased at this, and gave him another hundred *ashrafis*. " Sire," continued the old man, " others planted for us to eat ; we planted for others to eat, but we not only lived and ate ourselves, we even left something for our posterity to eat in comfort." The king was delighted with this answer, and gave the old man yet another hundred *ashrafis*. " Sire," began the old man—but at this juncture the king's chief minister, Bozorgmehr, interrupted. " Let us leave, Your Majesty, for if we expose ourselves much longer to the ready wit of this astute old man, the royal treasury will soon be empty." The proverb as used encourages one to look ahead and to plan for the future.

What is cheaply found is despised.

What is brought by the wind will be carried away by the wind.

One day the wind blew a cotton-seed into a sparrow's nest. He asked his neighbour what it was, and he replied, " If you sow this, it will produce a pod, the pod will produce cotton, the cotton will be spun into thread, the thread will be woven into cloth, the cloth will be dyed and sewn up into coats for you and me." The sparrow took the seed to a peasant in a field, saying, " Sow ! Sow ! Sow this seed ! Half for me and half for you." The peasant did so, and when after a while the plant came up and the pods were ripe, he divided them between himself and the sparrow. The sparrow took his share to the spinner, saying, " Spin ! Spin ! Spin this cotton ! Half for me and half for you." The spinner did so and gave the sparrow his share. The sparrow took the thread to the weaver, saying, " Weave ! Weave ! Weave this thread ! Half for me and half for you." The weaver did so and gave the sparrow his share. The sparrow took it to the dyer, saying, " Dye ! Dye ! Dye this cloth ! Half for me and half for you." The dyer dyed the cloth bright blue and hung it on the line to dry in the sun. When the sparrow saw it, he thought, " What a beautiful colour ! It seems a pity to divide such a fine piece of cloth." He swooped down and carried it off in his beak, and took it to the tailor, saying, " Sew ! Sew ! Sew this cloth ! One for you and one for me." So the tailor made two beautiful coats and hung them on a peg. The sparrow thought, " It seems a pity to give such a fine coat to the tailor. I'll take both for myself." So he snatched the two coats and took them to the *molla*, saying, " O *molla*, I wish to leave these two coats in trust with you, until such time as the weather gets colder. In return, one shall be for you, and one for me." The *molla* agreed, but to himself he thought, " It seems a pity to give one of these coats to this ridiculous sparrow. I'll keep both for myself." When the winter came, the sparrow came for his coat, but the *molla* claimed ignorance. " If you are cold, I will pray for you," he said. The sparrow flew off angrily, but from a distance he saw the *molla* washing the two coats and hanging them on the line. So when he was praying, the sparrow flew down and snatched the two coats, and took them to the bazaar to sell for food. On the way a storm blew up and whipped the two coats out of the sparrow's beak. No matter how he tried, he could not recover them. The wind carried them away and dropped one before the tailor and the other before the dyer. So justice was done.

Unless you take pains you will never acquire wealth.

Whoever needs a peacock must put up with a journey to India.

He who wants a rose must respect the thorn.

You will eat no more stew than you pay for.

I will only card cotton to the amount of your buttermilk.

You cannot expect something for nothing. Every gain requires an effort of some kind.

You must start by night to arrive by day.

To walk and sit is better than to run and burst.

The well-known story of the hare and the tortoise is often told in support of this proverb. Sa'di also has a story in his *Golestan*, in which he relates how, when a young man, he had been hurrying all day, and by evening was so exhausted that he could do no more than throw himself down against a bank at the side of the road. A feeble old man, who was following the caravan at leisure, said, "Why are you sitting? Get up, for this is no place to sleep." "How can I," I replied, "when I have no strength to walk?" "Haven't you heard," said the old man, "that it is better to walk and sit than to run and burst?"

Drops that gather one by one finally become a sea.

A verse from Naser-e Khosrou.

You must climb a ladder step by step.

A hasty man does his work twice over.

Compare the Arabic "Haste is from the Devil."

From fear of the porridge he fell into the pot.

More haste, less speed.

This is no task to be dipped in and out of a dye-vat.

Take your time over a task if you want to do it properly.

First raise this one child that you have borne.

Don't turn to another task before you have finished the first.

You can't get raisins without unripe grapes.

Don't pass on to the last stages of a task before completing the first.

Soft words will get the snake out of its hole.

Gentle methods are best.

The seeker at last becomes the finder.

With patience you may make halva *from unripe grapes.*

By constantly asking one can reach China.

Where there's a will there's a way.

Unless the child cries, how will it get milk?

A camel that wants fodder stretches out its neck.

Those who don't ask don't get.

God is the Provider, but he needs a nudge.

In other words, God helps those who help themselves. Two friends were disputing, one of them maintaining that God would provide all one's needs, the other arguing that one had to work for one's living. At length, to settle the matter, the first man went and sat in a corner of the mosque to wait his sustenance from God. Two days passed, and then three, and still nothing came from earth or heaven. But on the evening of the third day three villagers came into the mosque to eat their bread and cheese. As they were packing up the remainder of the food before leaving, our friend, seeing his last chance about to disappear, coughed gently. The villagers noticed him and, taking pity on his haggard appearance, gave him the remains of their food. The man went back to his friend in all humility. "God is indeed the Provider," he admitted, "but he needs a nudge."

Go and wake up your luck.

The same idea as the preceding. According to popular belief, a man's luck is personified by a man who sleeps from time to time.

A widely known story relates how there were two brothers, one rich and one poor. The latter tried one night to steal some of his brother's wheat, and was prevented by a man who turned out to be his brother's luck. This man told the poor brother that his luck was asleep on the top of a distant mountain, and advised him to go and wake him. On the way the brother met a lion, a horse and a tree (according to one version), all of whom posed questions for his luck to solve. He eventually found his luck, woke him, and got the answers to his three questions. The tree and the horse were satisfied with what they were told, but the lion had asked, "Why is it that, however much I eat, I am never satisfied?" The answer was that he should eat the brains of the most foolish man he could find. The lion looked at the brother and exclaimed, "I have never seen anyone as foolish as you," and promptly tore him in pieces.

A fish taken from the water is always fresh.

It's never too late to mend.

No one scratches my back but my own finger-nail.

If you want a job well done, do it yourself. Compare the three following.

The master's eye has its own effect.

A man went on a journey and left his favourite horse in the care of an old friend. The friend gave his grooms instructions to pay special attention to this horse, but in spite of this it languished from the first. He began to give it personal attention, but even though he spent all his time in the stable, the horse continued to waste away. He sent for the best horse-doctors, but all to no avail. It was all the more surprising because his own horse, though he neglected it, was fat and flourishing. Eventually the horse's owner returned from his journey. His friend confessed with shame that, in spite of all his care, the horse was sick and wasting. The owner smiled and replied, "Didn't you know that the master's eye has its own effect?"

A mother burns her heart, a nurse her apron.

The more closely you are concerned with something, the more trouble you take over it.

If I had been there, she would have had a son.

A man from the village of Sedeh near Isfahan went on a journey, and on his return was greeted with the news that his wife had borne him a daughter. "If I had been there," he grumbled, "she would have had a son."

He who sits and waits for his neighbour will sleep hungry.

Every man is king in his own house.

Four walls make a man free.

The dog is a lion in his own house.

Three proverbs with a similar meaning.

He who eats the bread of his hands has no need of Hatem Ta'i.

Hatem Ta'i was an Arab chieftain famed for his generosity. Sa'di tells how one day Hatem was giving a great feast to all the sheikhs and tribesmen in the neighbourhood and, happening to go out into the desert, came across a poor camel-herd. "Haven't you heard," he asked, "that Hatem Ta'i is giving a great feast for all who wish to come?" The camel-herd's reply has become proverbial.

It is better to die a beggar than to ask for help.

This verse, like the preceding and the two following, are from Sa'di's *Golestan*. A beggar was suffering the utmost extremities of hunger, and a passer-by said to him, "There is a man in this city who is renowned for his generosity. Why don't you go to him, for when he knows of your plight he will be sure to help you?" The beggar's reply, as a proverb, suggests that one should not be under an obligation to another.

One man honoured in death is better than a hundred living in shame.

To die with honour is better than to live in disgrace.

A courageous man received a terrible wound in the wars against the Tatars. He was told that a certain great man possessed a potent medicine ; however, this person was notorious for his avarice. The wounded man replied, " If I ask for the medicine, he may or may not give it ; and if he gives it, it may or may not benefit me. Begging from him would itself be poison, for whatever you beg from the mean may ſatten your body, but it will detract from your honour."

4. VIRTUE ITS OWN REWARD

Our next section starts with the theme that virtue is its own reward. Emphasis, however, is on the personal aspect; we must do good if we wish to receive good, and by extension we must cure our own faults before we criticize the faults of others. We are warned how easy it is to be blind to our own shortcomings, to be swayed by self-interest in coming to a decision. Justice should be based on fair shares for all; no innocent man should be blamed for the sins of others. Conversely, we must remember that our own evil actions may have repercussions on others, particularly on our own kindred.

Good deeds return to the house of their author.

Blood cannot be washed out with blood.

Two wrongs do not make a right.

Do to me what would please you if it were done to you.

Stick a needle into yourself before a bodkin into others.

Cast first the beam out of thine own eye.

She couldn't tidy her own head, but she went to dress the bride.

A lazy and slovenly woman, who would hardly budge from the corner of the room in order to fetch a jug of water, heard one day that a fine wedding was being held in the headman's house, and decided that at all costs she must go to it. Without even bothering to dress up, she shuffled along and sneaked into the house among the other guests. The hostess soon noticed her and, realizing that she was not one of the invited, asked her what she was doing there. "I am the lady's maid," she replied, "I've come to get the bride ready for the wedding and to tie the kerchief round her head." Another guest, who knew the woman for what she was, remarked, "If you're good at tying kerchiefs, why don't you tie one round your own head?" The implication of the proverb, like those that follow, is that one should attend to one's own faults first.

The doctor must heal his own bald head.[1]

If you mend water-bags, go and mend your own.

If you can sing lullabies, send yourself to sleep.

He was thrown out of the village, and he claimed the headman's house.

This proverb and the one that follows point to the unwisdom of trying to carry out a major task when you have proved incapable of completing a small one.

He who has no bread doesn't eat an onion.

An onion, that is, to stimulate his appetite.

No one sees his own faults.

Everyone sees his own image in the water; the farmer sees rain, the washerman sun.

Everyone sees what he wants to see.

The elephant dreams one thing, the elephant-driver another.

Everyone thinks of himself; even the thin-beard thinks of his beard.

[1] In Persia and many other parts of the Middle East baldness is the result of a scalp disease.

He who goes to the qazi *alone returns happy.*

A judge who hears only one side of the case cannot decide impartially. Similar thoughts are to be found in many of the great poets, particularly Nezami, Attar, Naser-e Khosrou and Rumi.

His verdict is like that of the qazi *of Balkh.*

Our donkey never had a tail!

These two proverbs come from the same story, both being protests against unfair decisions. A debtor was being dragged by his creditor to the *qazi* of Balkh, and hoping to escape dashed through the open door of a house and up the stairs on to the roof. Unfortunately for him there was no other way down, and in jumping into the neighbouring yard he landed on the neighbour's wife, who was pregnant. As a result she had a miscarriage, and the infuriated husband seized upon the debtor, who, seeing that " when the water has covered the head, a hundred fathoms are as one ", told him to join the creditor and see the *qazi*. A little further on a runaway horse was being chased. The debtor, trying to be helpful, threw a stone at it, and the stone " went everywhere " until it hit the horse in the eye, blinding it. The owner came up in a rage, and the debtor replied, " We are all on our way to the *qazi* ; you had better come with us." They came next to an overloaded ass that had fallen down in the mud, and its owner asked the four men for help. They all took hold of it, the debtor grasping the tail ; and as luck would have it, when he pulled, the tail came right off. The owner began to abuse the debtor, but the latter replied, " All right, you too had better come to the *qazi*." Finally they came to the *qazi's* house, and as they went in, the debtor secretly concealed a large stone under his coat. As he bowed to the *qazi*, he surreptitiously pointed to the bulge in his coat, implying that it was a purse of gold. The *qazi* took the hint, and then called on the creditor to state his case. The debtor flatly denied his claims, and since the creditor had no papers in support of them, the *qazi* sent him away empty-handed. Then the husband came forward and told his story. The *qazi* replied, " Very well, this woman must go and stay in the defendant's house until she is once more pregnant ; he must be liable for all her expenses, and during this period her husband must not come near her." The husband protested violently against this decision, and finally the *qazi* ruled that, in consideration of a payment of five hundred *rials* by the husband to the debtor, all claims and counter-claims between them should be cancelled. Next the horse-owner came forward, and the *qazi* said, " Certainly the defendant must pay damages, but in order that we may assess them fairly, the horse is to be sawn in half, and the half with the sound eye sold in the bazaar ; whatever price it fetches will be a fair valuation of the half that the defendant has damaged." The owner protested violently, and finally it was decided that the debtor should receive a sum of one hundred *rials* from the horse-owner and should keep the horse. Meanwhile the owner of the donkey had been watching all this with growing concern, and when his turn came, he tried to sneak out of the court. The *qazi* called after him, " Where are you going, my friend? Come and state your case." But the donkey's owner replied, " I have no complaint, your honour ; I swear that my donkey never had a tail, even as a colt ! "

It's the story of the mouse and the slab of cheese.

Two mice one day stole a piece of cheese and, being unable to agree over the division of it, decided to take the case to an old cat, who had long since repented of her ways and given up chasing mice. " Certainly," agreed the cat, " I will divide it fairly for you." She took a knife and cut the cheese into two unequal halves. She then placed them in the scales and, finding that they did not balance, cut a piece off the larger and swallowed it. It was now the other half that was too heavy, and so she repeated the process. This went on until finally there was only a tiny piece left in one of the scales. " And this," she said, gobbling it up, " is my fee ! "

One roof and two climates !

Another proverb on the subject of unfair discrimination. It is generally said that mothers-in-law are well-disposed to their sons-in-law and ill-disposed to their daughters-in-law. It so happened that a mother was living in the same house as her son and daughter and their respective wife and husband. It was towards the end of summer, and people were still sleeping on the roof at night. One night the mother woke, and as it seemed that the night had turned a little cold, she went over to her sleeping daughter and her husband and pulled the quilt over them, saying, " The night has turned a little cold, you must be careful of yourselves." Then she went over to her son and daughter-in-law and pulled back the covers, saying, " You really shouldn't use so many bedclothes in this hot weather, you will make yourselves ill." Her daughter-in-law, who had been awake and heard all that had passed, cried out in astonishment, " Good heavens, one roof and two climates! That side is cold and this is hot."

The mill-wheel turns.

First come, first served ; turn and turn about. The image is taken from peasants bringing their grain to the mill to be ground.

Injustice all round is justice.

Compare the Arabic, " Evil is good if it is shared."

This is the shrine that we built together.

A certain dervish had a group of followers, one of whom persistently refused to recognize his authority. One day they were in a remote part of the desert, and while the other disciples were preparing a meal, the rebellious one was amusing himself in burying the bones of a donkey that he had found there. The dervish watched him for a while, and then came over and helped him to build a mound and place a stone over the spot, so that it looked like a real grave. Then he asked the rebellious disciple, " Are you ready yet to acknowledge my authority?" " No," replied the disciple. So the dervish called his other followers together and told them to tie him up against the mound that they had built. " We shall leave you here," he said,

" the wild beasts will come and devour you, and finally some travellers will find you and bury you in this grave together with that unclean donkey." Then they went off, and the unfortunate disciple was left there in fear and trembling. At last with a great effort he worked himself up against the stone on top of the grave, and by dint of rubbing managed to cut through the cord that bound his hands. Just at that moment he heard the bells of a distant caravan and, lighting a torch, he stood on top of the mound and finally attracted the attention of the merchants. " What are you doing in this desolate place?" they asked in amazement as they came up. " Three days ago," replied the youth, " I came to this tomb and lay down to rest. In my dreams I saw a revered *sayed* who said, ' This grave is the grave of one of the martyrs of our family, who suffered death in this desert. You who have found your way here must spare no effort to preserve it from destruction.' So here I have remained for three days and nights braving all hardships." The merchants, impressed with the youth's piety and devotion, each gave him food and money, and went on their way. Soon the news spread throughout the neighbouring villages and towns, and pilgrims began to come from far and wide to the newly-discovered tomb, bringing gifts of all kinds. Before long the youth was able to have a dome built over the grave, and after two or three years the whole face of the desert was changed, with mosques, shrines and cloisters, and a fine palace and servants for the youth himself, who now styled himself the " Custodian of the Shrine ". Seven years passed, and by chance the same dervish came with his followers to that spot, and was astonished at the change that had taken place. The Custodian observed and recognized them, and ordered that they should be lavishly entertained for a week. On the eighth day the Custodian himself came to the dervish's lodging, but though the dervish recognized his face, he could not think where he had met him before. The Custodian gradually worked the conversation round to his own story, and related how he had come there seven years before with a dervish, how they had camped there, and how he and the dervish " had built this shrine together ". The dervish at last recognized his former disciple and, falling on his knees, begged forgiveness.

The proverb is generally used nowadays by someone who feels that his partner in an undertaking is trying to take all the profit.

The donkey works and the horse eats.

The camel-driver reaps where the muleteer sowed.

Two proverbs used when one person does all the work and someone else takes all the profit or credit.

He couldn't manage the ass, so he pilfered its saddle.

Said when someone takes out his anger with a powerful man on someone weaker than himself.

Every month is dangerous, but Safar has the bad name.

Safar, the second of the Moslem months, is regarded as particularly unlucky. In Bedouin times fighting was forbidden during the three preceding months, and hence a great many men generally lost their lives in the renewed hostilities of Safar. It is also said that nine-tenths of all diseases come during Safar. The proverb is equivalent to "Give a dog a bad name . . ."

Money goes to one place, suspicion to a thousand.

When one person steals, many innocent men may be suspected.

They don't unload the caravan for one lame donkey.

They don't close the mosque for one menstruating woman.[1]

They don't set the bazaar on fire for a handkerchief.

A haberdasher's apprentice was just closing the shop for the day, when his sweetheart came in for a chat. She noticed on the shelf two

[1] A menstruating woman may not pray.

beautifully embroidered handkerchiefs ; " the pot of her greed came to the boil ", and she begged the apprentice to give them to her. " I can't do that," he replied ; " only the master may sell those ; it's as much as my life is worth to touch them, for ' there's a snake sitting on them '." But the girl insisted, and finally the boy agreed. When she had gone, he came to his senses. " He'll never believe me if I say they're lost, and if I tell him they're sold he'll want the money, and if I say I sold them on credit he'll answer that that's forbidden, and if I say that I've bought them myself, where will I find the money to pay for them ? " Finally he bethought himself of a mischievous idea ; he started a fire in the corner of the shop and, locking the door, hurried off. Before long the fire spread to the neighbouring shops ; and by the time it was discovered, it was too late to control it, and in the end the whole bazaar was destroyed.

An injured hand means trouble for the neck.

A man's misfortunes bring grief to his relatives.

The oppressor's wrongs fall on his children's heads.

5. *MISERS AND SKINFLINTS*

In this section we come to the engrossing subject of miserliness and its accompanying vices of envy, covetousness and greed. Many are the stories told of misers; perhaps one of the most typical is of the three who were trying to outdo one another. " I'm so mean," said the first, " that if someone knocks at the door when I'm about to start my supper, I hastily clear it away so that I won't have to share it." " Oh, that's nothing," retorted the second, " that only means that you haven't enough to go round. Now I'm so mean that, when I go out to a dinner-party, I object if another guest turns up." " That's not real meanness," laughed the third, " you're just afraid that your host didn't know this other guest was coming, and will only have prepared food for two. Now I'm really mean. If someone gives me a present, I get angry with him for wasting his substance! " A man like this, we are told, could " get colour from water ", he would " put the cat in prison ", he could " let a fly's blood in the air ". Even " water will not drip from his hand ". But there is a consoling thought. Pride comes before a fall, and so it will be with all skinflints and those who oppress the poor and weak; their " drum will be torn ", " their wash-tub will fall from the roof".

He dedicated spilt oil to the shrine.

One day a man was passing in front of a shrine with a jar of oil in his hand. Suddenly it slipped, and all the oil was spilt. The man turned towards the shrine and called out, " O holy saint, I dedicate this oil to your lamps! " The proverb is used of a selfish person who gives away something worthless.

He gives a party with the bath-water.

The sheikh succumbed to the broth.

The headman of the village wanted the *molla* to endorse some fictitious document for him. So he invited him to dine, and instructed his wife to prepare an excellent meal and to take particular care with a special kind of broth, of which the *molla* was very fond since he had no teeth. The *molla* duly arrived, enjoyed a pipe and a glass of tea, and as they had expected, did full justice to the excellent broth. He finished off with another glass of tea and a pipe, and then without further ado rose to his feet and prepared to leave. The headman, greatly upset, begged and implored him to stay a little longer, but the *molla* would not hear of it and with a thousand excuses took his leave and departed. " Didn't the sheikh like the broth ? " asked the headman's wife. " Yes," said her husband. " Then why didn't he sign the document ? " " Alas," replied the headman, " the sheikh succumbed to the broth." The proverb is now used of someone who is only co-operative up to the point where he has secured all he wants.

What pauper hasn't a tuman *in his pocket ?*

A certain merchant used to send his black slave to collect his accounts, but wherever he went, he would get the reply, " I have no money," and being a simple fellow he believed them. The merchant realized that, because the slave had never himself had any money in his pocket, he thought that everyone else was the same. So he gave him a *tuman's* worth of small change, and told him always to carry it with him ; and in future whenever the slave met with a negative response, he would answer, " What pauper hasn't at least a *tuman* in his pocket ? " The proverb is used in reference to an obdurate creditor who will not take " no " for an answer.

The " haves " know nothing of the " have-nots ".

The full man knows nothing of the hungry, nor the rider of the walker.

He who sits on the fence is light of heart.

He'll let it rot for the dog before he shares it with another.

Said of a " dog in the manger ".

The neighbour's morsel has goose-fat on it.

Other people's possessions always seem better than one's own.

The blind man is laughing at the baldhead.

The pot is calling the kettle black, or, as the Persians themselves also put it,

One pot calls another black.

The blind man thinks that the seeing man eats with both hands.

Said of someone who envies others without due cause.

There are many walnuts in the qazi's *house, but they are all counted.*

It is useless to envy other people's wealth.

The molla *who lives free ought to marry the mice in the house.*

A scrounger should do something in return for what he gets.

No one has ever seen the leg of a snake, the eye of an ant, or charity from a molla.

He wants both God and dates.

He wants to have his cake and eat it. According to tradition, the Dajjal (equivalent to the Antichrist) will appear before the end of the world mounted on a monstrous donkey, which will drop dates instead of dung. Men will follow the Dajjal for the sake of the dates and will be led into Hell.

His pot died in childbirth.

Said of someone who suffers loss because of his greed. Molla Nasr ad-Din one day borrowed a pot from his neighbour, and the next day returned it with a little pot inside. "This little pot isn't mine," said his neighbour. "Yes, it is," replied the *molla*, "your pot gave birth to it last night." The neighbour, a greedy man, thought to take advantage of Molla Nasr ad-Din's simplicity and said no more. A few days later the *molla* borrowed the pot again; but this time several days passed, and the pot was not returned. So the neighbour went round to ask for it; but the *molla* greeted him with a long face and said, "Alas! Your pot died in childbirth." "What are you talking about?" exclaimed the angry neighbour. "Well, you weren't surprised when I told you the other day that it had given birth, so why should you be surprised now?"

He smells kabobs, but it's only a roasting donkey.

Said of someone who blunders through excessive greed.

Even the qazi *will drink free wine.*

Most men will sacrifice principle for greed.

A hungry man has no faith.

A man was nearly dying of hunger. The Devil came to him and offered him food if the man would sell him his faith. The hungry man agreed, but when he had eaten his fill he refused, saying, "What I sold you when I was hungry did not exist, for a hungry man has no faith."

To the hungry wolf good camel-meat or the Dajjal's donkey are all one.

A verse from Sa'di with a meaning similar to that of the preceding proverb.

Even a single hair from a bear is profit.

It is worth while getting anything from a miser.

A fat dog would become a greyhound in his house.

A man dined one evening at the house of the village headman; but the latter was an excessively mean man, and not only gave him a very poor meal, but provided none of the amenities that might be expected from a host. A few days later the guest was present with a number of other elders of the village at a meeting in the headman's house, when the headman caught sight of a large and well-fed stray dog. "I must catch that dog," he said, "he will make an excellent watch-dog for my house." "For goodness' sake don't do that," protested the guest; "in your house it won't be long before he turns into a greyhound."

Don't get hit on the head with your basin.

An avaricious man went one day to the public bath. Alone in the changing-room, he began to bemoan his hard lot and, praying to God, said, "O God, before anyone else comes please fill this changing-room with *ashrafis*, that my wretched lot may change." He remained for a few minutes with his hands raised, but no matter how long he dawdled over his undressing, not a single *ashrafi* appeared. At last he moved on into the hot bath, and there again prayed, saying, "O God, perhaps the changing-room was too large, but could you not at least fill this smaller room?" But again nothing happened, and he went on into a yet smaller room and offered up a similar prayer, but with equally little effect. Finally he came out into the courtyard and, filling his basin with water, placed it before him and prayed, "O God, it seems that those three other places were too large, but could you not at least fill this little basin with *ashrafis*? If you won't do that, then hit me on the head with it, so that at any rate, if I can't enjoy your favour, I may suffer your disfavour." It so happened that a mischievous fellow in the bath had overheard the whole story, and creeping up behind the miser he seized the basin, hit him on the head with it and ran off before the unfortunate man came to. The miser raised his hands in protest. "O God," he cried, "you were deaf to all my appeals to fill the bath with *ashrafis*, but the moment

I asked you to hit me on the head with my basin, your hearing became as sharp as could be!" The proverb is used as a warning against greed and also, satirically, to someone who has asked in vain from a miser.

A stone is as good as gold for hiding.

This story comes from the *Bustan* of Sa'di. A miser hoarded all his wealth and spent nothing on his family. But one day his son discovered the hiding-place, and he dug up all the gold and put a large stone in its place. The money he spent in riotous living. His father soon discovered his loss, and was overcome with grief; but his son said cheerfully, "Gold is for spending, father; for hiding, a stone is just as good."

He eats his cheese in a bottle.

A miser, after much heart-searching, spent a single *shahi* on a small piece of cheese to go with his bread. But as he was about to swallow it, he thought, "If I eat this now, I shall have only to spend another *shahi* to-morrow. I have a much better idea." He put the cheese in a bottle and corked it up firmly, and whenever mealtime came round, he tore off a piece of bread, rubbed it on the bottle, and ate it with great relish. In this way he was able to make that same piece of cheese last for years without any further expense.

The potter drinks water from a broken pot.

The lamp does not light its own base.

Both these imply that men are least generous to themselves and those nearest to them.

It is easy to be Hatem Ta'i with the guest's money.

Reference has already been made to Hatem Ta'i. The proverb indicates that it is easy to be liberal in spending someone else's money.

A dog is better than an oppressor of men.

A verse from Sa'di.

He has bound Shemr's hand behind his back.

Shemr was the murderer of Hosein at Kerbela, and ever since he has figured as an object of Shi'ite execration in the annual "passion plays" in Moharram. The proverb implies that So-and-so has outdone Shemr in cold-blooded cruelty.

A knife would not draw his blood.

Said of a harsh, cold-blooded man.

God knew the donkey and would not give him horns.

Ignorant people are likely to abuse their power. Sa'di wrote, "If the donkey had had two horns like the cow, he wouldn't have left one man's stomach unpierced."

If you hit it again, I shall have nothing.

A man had a load of glass vessels on the back of a donkey, and was taking them out to market through the main gate of a city. An official stopped him and, smacking the bundle with a stick, asked, "What have you got there?" The man replied, "If you hit it again, I shall have nothing." The proverb implies that there is a limit to anyone's power to endure oppression. There may even be a slight suggestion of "killing the goose that laid the golden eggs".

Couldn't you find a wall lower than ours?

You are oppressing us because we are the humblest persons you can find.

He who ill-treats his mother will do worse to another.

You should avoid dealings with a man who permits ill-treatment of those nearest to him.

When the snake is old, the frog will tease him.

When a powerful man falls, no one has respect for him any more.

Kindness to evil men is as bad as injury to good men.

Sa'di has two verses which themselves have almost become proverbs: "Harshness in return for harshness is an act of justice," and "To spare the ravening leopard is an act of injustice to the sheep."

Snakes bite everyone, cockroaches bite snakes.

A warning to one who torments those weaker than himself.

Above every hand there are other hands.

Everyone has his superior. An Arabic proverb says, "Above every hand is the hand of God, and every oppressor will himself be oppressed."

When the fountain has gone up, it comes down.

Pride comes before a fall.

Winter has passed, but coal still has a black face.

A man's face is said to be blackened when he is shamed. Another form of the proverb attributes the black face to "the coal-merchant", and the expression is used by someone who has survived an ordeal, in spite of the failure of others to help him. A similar idea is implied in the proverb that follows.

The night in sable has passed, and so has the night by the ovenside.

It is related that Soltan Mahmud of Ghazné, having spent the evening in feasting, slept the rest of the night in covers of sable. A poor beggar also passed the night by the side of the oven. When morning came the beggar cried out to the soltan, "The night in sable has passed, and so has the night by the ovenside!" In other words, although you did nothing to help me, you are this morning no better off than I am.

6. THE FOLLY OF BOASTING

There is a tendency for proverbs to tilt against existing human failings rather than to set up new heights for man to attain. So in this section again the emphasis is on vice rather than virtue. This time we are warned against the haughty and obstinate, against those who have " wind in the head ", who are " Arab from the roots " (an odd sidelight on the relations between the Persians and their Arab neighbours); to have dealings with such people is like " going into a sack with a bear ". Nor is there a good word to be said for officious meddlers, people who " stick their fingers in the milk ". As for the boasters, those who " throw wind into their sleeves ", who " throw dried-up straw to the wind ", they will soon be exposed. We cannot, so we are repeatedly warned, escape the consequences of our actions. This is a favourite theme among the classical writers, and this fact itself is a reflection of its prevalence in popular lore.

It's an obstinate ass that will gladly die to harm its master.

Compare " to cut off one's nose to spite one's face ".

I'll let go of the bladder, but the bladder won't let go of me.

Some friends were out rowing on a lake, and in the distance saw something floating on the water. One of them said, " It looks like a bladder of syrup," and when the others laughed at him, he pulled off his coat and jumped into the water in order to fetch it. But when he got nearer he suddenly realized that it was a bear that had fallen into the lake and was trying to swim out. He turned away in haste, but the bear, at its last gasp, grabbed hold of his feet and hung on for dear life. Meanwhile the man's friends, tired of waiting, called, " Come back ! What do you want that bladder of syrup for ? " " I'll let go of the bladder," he retorted, " but the bladder won't let go of me." The proverb is used by someone who is plagued by an obstinate man or an obstinate problem.

The bowl is hotter than the stew.

Said of someone who sticks obstinately to an outmoded opinion, who is " more Catholic than the Pope ". It is sometimes also used in a sense equivalent to " Blood is thicker than water."

A blind man who sees is better than a seeing man who is blind.

There are none so deaf as those who won't hear.

The goose has only one foot.

Molla Nasr ad-Din one day took a roast goose as a present to a newly arrived governor. On the way he succumbed to the temptation of pulling off one of the legs and eating it. When he presented it to the governor, the latter noticed that one leg was missing. " What has happened to the other leg ? " he asked. " In this part of the world," said the *molla*, " the geese have only one leg. If you don't believe me, look out of the window at the geese by the pond." The governor looked out, and sure enough the geese were standing there on one leg. But just then some boys came along and began to chase them with sticks. " You liar ! " exclaimed the governor. " All those geese have two legs." " If you'd been chased with a stick like that," retorted the *molla*, " you'd have doubled the number of your legs." The proverb is used nowadays of someone who obstinately sticks to a statement, even when it has been proved untrue.

Wherever there is stew, So-and-so is the butler.

Said of an officious person who is always to be found where he is not wanted.

The onion has mixed itself with the fruit.

Someone has joined a group of people more important than himself.

The mosque is no place to dance.

The mosque is no place to tie one's donkey.

One must always consider the occasion.

Mint always grows green outside a snake's hole.

Said when a man is always running into someone he dislikes. Snakes are said to have an aversion to mint. An Arabic saying runs, "He is more loathsome than the smell of wild rue to snakes," a parallel idea.

The colt has gone ahead of its mother.

The part has become more important than the whole. Fools rush in where angels fear to tread. It is sometimes said of an officious and sycophantic person, "Have you only gone ahead in order not to be left behind?"

Hear a few words from the mother of the bride.

Said caustically to someone who speaks without being asked.

I speak to the door, but the wall may listen.

If the cap fits, wear it.

Self-praise is like chewing cotton-wool.

Musk is known by its smell, not by the shopkeeper's words.

Good wine needs no bush. Compare :

The bride whom her mother praises will do for her uncle.

The lamp has no brilliance in front of the sun.

A pompous man is shown at his true worth in the company of a great man. Compare :

A fake in the jewellers' bazaar is not worth a grain of barley.

A tall minaret is nothing beside Mount Alvand.

Don't use words too big for your mouth.

A large stone will never be thrown.
High-sounding threats seldom come to anything.

A hollow drum makes a great noise.

The big drum only sounds well from afar.
Virtues attributed to strangers seldom bear closer inspection.

The ugliest monkey shows off the most.
The meanest people make the biggest claims. Compare :

The goat-herd drinks from the source.

If he'd had some water, he'd have been a good swimmer.
It is easy to boast when your claims cannot be disproved. This is an idea that has inspired a number of stories and proverbs. Compare the following :

Yazd is far, yards are near.
A man from Yazd came on a visit to Isfahan, and boasted to some acquaintances that in Yazd he had jumped a distance of ten yards. One of his hearers observed, " Yazd is far, yards are near." Another story of the same proverb is as follows : A Yazdi weaver came to Isfahan to work in a factory and, although he never wove more than four yards a day, he would boast, " In Yazd I used to weave ten yards

a day." At length his employer cried out in exasperation, "Yazd is far, yards are near."

Beiza is far, nine donkeys are near.

A man from Beiza, on a visit to Shiraz, boasted that in his own town he had lined up nine donkeys nose to tail and jumped clear over them. A hearer remarked, "Beiza is far, nine donkeys are near."

Here is the ball and here the field.

A phrase used when inviting a boastful man to put his cards on the table. Many other expressions of the kind are used, including : Here is the well and here the rope, here is the seed and here the soil, here is the corpse and here the graveyard, here is the weight and here the scales, here is the weight and here the counter-weight, here is the mosque and here the pulpit, here is the goat and here the thief. In other words, here are all the factors in the case, now prove your claims.

The crow tried to copy the partridge's walk and forgot his own.

This story is told by Jami. A crow, being fond of comfort, decided to move his nest from the fields to a garden. His eye eventually lighted on one at the edge of the mountains, and in it was a handsome partridge hopping and strutting among the rocks and trees. The crow was greatly taken with this way of walking, and decided to imitate it. But after three or four days he had not only failed to imitate the partridge successfully, he had also forgotten his own style of walking. The Bakhtiyaris tell a similar story about a sparrow and a goose.

May he who does not see be blind!

Two geese and a tortoise shared a well. One day, as the water was getting low, the geese decided to fly away to another place. The tortoise begged them to take him too, and so the two geese grasped a stick in their beaks and told the tortoise to grip the middle of it with his teeth. After warning him not on any account to open his mouth, they took off. People below were astonished at this unusual sight, and began to shout and comment on it. The tortoise listened for a while, becoming more and more inflated with vanity, till a length he could contain himself no longer and cried out, " May he who does not see be blind ! " Instantly he fell to the ground and was dashed to pieces.

It's the same donkey, only his saddle has been changed.

Said of someone who has recently gained a high position—or sometimes of someone who is wearing a new suit !

A tumble-down bath-house doesn't need ten attendants.

A pennyworth of liver doesn't need a print tablecloth.

He has no dinner or supper, but he keeps seven jugs and basins

Three proverbs about people who keep up appearances beyond their means. The jug and basin is used for washing hands after a meal.

Do not ignore the retribution of your deeds ; you will reap wheat from wheat, barley from barley.

You may sow thorns, but you won't reap jasmine.

For what you have done yourself there is no remedy.

I was burnt with the fire that I myself lighted.

A miller was hard at work one day, when a demon from the desert came and sat in a corner of the mill. The miller asked him, " What is your name?" The demon replied, "What is your name?" The miller answered, "I am 'I myself'." The demon said, "I too am 'I myself'." The miller tried hard to think of some way of getting rid of this unwelcome visitor, but could hit on nothing. What he found especially annoying was that the demon copied everything he did; if he drank water, the demon drank water; if he ate bread, the demon did so; if he said something, the demon repeated the exact words. At last he had an idea. He fetched two basins, one full of water and the other of kerosene, and placed the first at one end of the mill. The demon promptly took the basin of kerosene to the other end. The miller then laid a box of matches in front of his basin and, splashing himself all over, struck a match and held it to his clothes. The demon went through the same actions, and at once burst into flames. The other demons in the desert heard his cries and came running to his aid. "Who did this to you?" they asked. "'I myself' did it," he cried. "But why should you do that?" they exclaimed. "I myself didn't do it, 'I myself' did it," replied the demon. "Well, there's no remedy for what you have done yourself," they retorted; and they went off and left him to burn to death. The proverb is now used of someone who has suffered the effects of his own folly, or sometimes too of someone who has fallen into the trap that he was preparing for someone else.

This is the bread that I baked for myself.

Dig a well for no one, for you will fall in first.

The well-digger is always at the bottom of his well.

Finger by finger do not take, lest you lose vat by vat.

A wealthy merchant, who had made a fortune in the sale of oil, used to instruct his assistant to tip the scales with his finger in the appropriate direction when buying or selling. "What is the purpose of cheating like that," asked the assistant, "for the sake of such a small profit?" "Haven't you heard, my boy," answered the merchant, "that 'drops that gather one by one finally become a sea'?" One day the merchant decided to journey from his home town of Baku to Persia, where, so he had heard, oil was fetching a good price. He packed his oil in vats and set sail with his assistant. On the way he began to talk of how, with the profits from his business, he would settle down in Persia, the land of his ancestors, buy a fine estate, and spend the rest of his days in peace and comfort. The words were hardly out of his mouth when a great storm began to blow up. Soon the vessel was being lashed by the waves, and the terrified merchant fell on his knees and began to pray. Just then the captain of the ship came up. "This is no time to weep and wail," he exclaimed, "we must find a way to lighten the ship. Our only hope is to throw overboard this cargo of oil of yours." In the extremity of his fear the merchant agreed, and even himself helped the sailors to throw the vats into the sea. The assistant looked at him slyly and said, "Finger by finger do not take, lest you lose vat by vat."

The stick of God is soundless, but its blows cannot be healed.

The mills of God grind slowly . . . Compare:

God seizes late, but seizes harshly.

A single stone is enough for a house of glass.

"People who live in glass houses . . ." Since glass was not used widely in Persia, this may be a reverse importation from Europe. The line occurs in the works of the sixteenth-century poet Zolali of Khonsar, the complete verse running, "In this world a whip is enough for a madman, and a stone for a house of glass."

Everyone drinks the water of his own heart.

Everyone's life is determined by what is within himself.

Compare:

God gives to each according to the measure of his heart.

You will take back with the hand with which you give.

The mud that you throw will fall on your own head.

7. TOO MANY COOKS . . .

We now come to the people who are most commonly the butt of popular wit—the fools, the incompetent, the man who " takes the donkey on to the roof", who " pounds water in a mortar ", who tries to " weigh the wind ". Such a man has obviously " eaten a donkey's brains ". It is certain that he will be left with nothing but " wind in his hand ". He might as well " crack a hollow walnut " or " take caraway seeds to Kerman ". " His arrow will strike a stone ", and it will be evident to all that he is " talking with his foot in the air ". And so we pass on to the improvident, the idlers, the infatuated and the daydreamers, those who waste their time " cooking raw dreams ", who " sleep on all four sides ", who indeed slumber so long and soundly that " in their dreams they see seven kings ". To those who try to excuse their conduct, the proverbs have an answer too, for by seeking to justify themselves they will only give the truth away.

A house with two mistresses will be deep in dust.

The village with two headmen falls into ruin.

Two midwives will twist the baby's head.

With two cooks the stew will be salty or tasteless.

A crowded reservoir breaks many jars.

The poet Mas'ud Sa'd Salman complained, " The heart is troubled when there are two loved ones ; the head is overweighted with two crowns ; wine in two cups brings drunkenness . . ." The Arabs say, " The ship that has two captains will sink."

He tried to pick out an eyelash and blinded his eye.

He only made things worse by his incompetence.

You've planted half with cotton-wool, now let me plant the rest with silk.

A novice at barbering was shaving a man's head, and every time he nicked it he put a little piece of cotton-wool on the spot. The unfortunate customer, growing restive, asked what was going on. "Oh, it's nothing," replied the barber, "I'm just planting cotton-wool." The enraged customer seized the mirror and, observing his ridiculous appearance, said, "All right, leave the rest, I want to plant silk!" The proverb is used when relieving someone of a task for which he is incompetent.

He is learning barbering on someone's bald head.

Said of a novice who is a nuisance to those he practises on.

Hasan seldom went to work, and when he did he went on Friday.

Friday is the Moslem day of rest. The proverb is used of a muddled and incompetent person.

A mouse could steal groats from his pocket.

Said of an incompetent man.

The fool's answer is silence.

In the mountains the bear is Avicenna.

Any fool can appear wise where there is no competition.

If you marry the donkey, you must carry its load.

If you associate with a fool, you must be prepared to put up with his folly.

The half-wit spoke, and the brainless one believed him.

Only a fool could believe such nonsense.

It's a wise man that laughs at his own iokes.

While there are fools in the world, no one will be in want.

A crow was sitting on the branch of a tree with a large piece of cheese in his beak. A fox came along and began to address him in a fawning voice. " May God have mercy upon your respected father! What a beautiful voice he had! How moved I was when he closed his eyes and piped a tune more beautiful than the nightingale's! But why should we grieve? If the father has gone, the son remains. What pleasure and pride it would be for me if you too would honour and delight us with notes like those your dear father used to sing." The foolish crow fell into the trap, closed his eyes, and opened wide his beak in order to sing. The cheese fell to the ground, and the fox seized it and ran off.

A long beard is a mark of folly.

An old scholar one day came upon the following saying in one of his books of learning: " A beard longer than a hand's breadth is a mark of folly." " How can this be?" he said to himself. " What has a man's beard to do with his intelligence? My own beard is several hands' breadth long, but no one can say that I am a fool. No, it is the writer who is a fool . . . All the same, even if the saying isn't true, there would be no harm in shortening my beard to one hand's breadth." So he reached for his scissors, but could not find them in his pen-case. " Never mind," he said, " the candle will do as well as a pair of scissors." He grasped his beard tightly one hand's breadth below his chin, and set fire to it with the candle. The flames soon spread to his hand, and with a cry of pain he let go; before he could extinguish the blaze, his beard was gone and his face badly burned. When he returned from hospital, he turned to that same page and wrote in the margin, " I have personally tested this saying, it is quite true."

Where the heart is, there is happiness.

He has fallen in love with the eyes of the frog.

Some thirsty merchants in the desert came to a well, but found to their dismay that when they let a bucket down, it did not come up again. Several of their number also climbed down, but none of them returned. One of the merchants had a sly and clever servant, whom he instructed to go down the well. The servant naturally refused, but when the other merchants promised him a great reward, he finally agreed and, tying a rope round his waist, was lowered into the well. When he got to the bottom, he found a demon squatting in a corner, with his eyes firmly fixed on a large frog in the other corner. The servant immediately bowed low and paid his respects in the most courteous manner. The demon said, " If you had failed to greet me, like those other mortals, I would have swallowed you whole. Now I have a question that you must answer correctly before I will let you take any water. Where is happiness to be found?" Now the servant had noticed how the demon's eyes were fixed on the frog, and he answered, " Where the heart is, there is happiness." The demon was so pleased with this reply that he said to the servant, " Bravo! Now go through that door into the garden that you will find, and pick yourself ten pomegranates. Keep them carefully, for in each one you will find treasure enough to keep you for the rest of your days. Then call out to your friends, that they may pull up the bucket and you with it." This is an episode in a much longer story, the details of which do not concern us here. The proverb is now used of someone who is infatuated with something worthless.

What is held in the heart seems good to the eye.

Beauty is in the eye of the beholder. Sa'di relates how a certain wise man was asked why it was that, although Soltan Mahmud of Ghazné had many beautiful slaves in his *andarun*, he paid none of them so much attention as he did to his favourite Ayaz, who was no beauty. He replied, " What is held in the heart seems good to the eye."

Leila must be seen through Majnun's eyes.

Leila and Majnun are the heroine and hero of the Persian equivalent of the Romeo and Juliet story; several of the great Persian poets have been inspired by their tragedy.

He hasn't time to scratch his head.

He hasn't time to divorce his wife.

These two sayings are used of a man who is too preoccupied to attend to anything, however important. The story is told of a Shirazi who married an Isfahani wife. The Shirazis are noted for their indolence and light-hearted ways, and this man was no exception. His new wife, a typically shrewd and practical Isfahani, determined to reform him. "You really mustn't sit around all day like that," she said, "I'll find you a nice easy occupation." So the next morning she cooked a large bowl of stew and told him to sit comfortably on the front doorstep and sell it to the passers-by. When that task was working satisfactorily, she said, "Now we must arrange something for your afternoons." She gave him a large fodder-bag and said, "Walk slowly round the streets, taking care not to tire yourself, and collect all the dung that you can find." A few days later she arranged for him to spend his evenings cooking beets over the furnace of the bath-house and selling them to the patrons. So it went on, and after a week or two the unfortunate Shirazi found every minute of his day occupied; "he hadn't even time to scratch his head". One day, when he was out collecting dung, he met an old friend and, without stopping his work, began to complain to him of his hard lot. "A wife like that is no good," replied his friend. "Why don't you divorce her?" "I haven't even time for that," lamented the Shirazi.[1]

There is so much trefoil that you can't see the jasmine.

Said to a man who claims to be too busy to attend to minor matters.

[1] Under Islamic law it is sufficient for a husband to declare three times before witnesses, "I divorce her."

You can't pick up two melons with one hand.

If you have too many preoccupations, you will succeed at none of them. Compare :

One place is everywhere, everywhere is nowhere.

Shoes wear out with too much running.

When you sang so loud, you never thought of the winter.

A nightingale and an ant lived in a garden, the former on the highest branch of a tall tree, the latter in a small hole at its foot. The nightingale spent its days and nights in flying round the garden and singing, while the ant busied itself in adding to its store. The ant watched the nightingale flirting with the rose and said to itself, "Time will tell a different story." Autumn came, the flowers withered, and the leaves turned yellow ; the nightingale found itself friendless and hungry. In this predicament it thought of the ant, and decided to appeal to it as a good neighbour. In all humility it acknowledged its improvident ways and begged for help. But the ant said sternly, "When you sang so loud, you never thought of the winter." And it reminded the nightingale of the proverb :

Every spring has an autumn and every road an ending.

He bought what was useless and sold what was needful.

A certain man sold a piece of land and bought a horse. A friend said to him, "You have sold that which gave you barley and have bought that which will consume it."

The bride cannot go out if she has no veil.

You must make sure that you have all the facilities that you need before you embark on a task.

You can't mend father's grave with bits and pieces.

Two brothers came to visit their father's grave, and found it in great disrepair. The elder said, "We must put this in order. Go into that old tomb and see if you can't find some bricks we can use." The younger brother went into the tomb and brought out all the whole bricks he could find, but they were not nearly enough. He went a second time and brought a load of the largest broken pieces he could find, but still there was not enough. The third time he was obliged to bring an armful of chips and shavings, and as he threw them down he said, "You can't mend father's grave with bits and pieces." The proverb implies that it is a waste of time to set about a task with inadequate tools and materials.

A wedding in the bridegroom's house, but nothing in the bride's.

Said when someone acts without thinking and before the proper time.

Keep the lamp for darkness.

Don't waste your possessions. Keep them for when you need them.

White gold for a black day.

Something laid by for a rainy day.

You may buy a mouse-hole for a hundred dinars.

The mouse-hole is a way of escape, and the idea is that it is wise to keep something in reserve, not to burn your boats, and so on.

He is like the servant of the aubergine.

One day Nasr ad-Din Shah was eating a dish of aubergines and, turning to his chamberlain, remarked, "What an excellent vegetable the aubergine is!" "Yes, indeed, Your Majesty," replied the chamberlain; "it is the most delicious of vegetables. It is at once appetizing, nourishing and tasty." The next day His Majesty, having over-indulged his appetite the day before, was suffering from a stomach-ache and observed, "What an unpleasant vegetable the aubergine is . . ." The chamberlain broke in, "Yes, indeed, Your Majesty, the aubergine is the worst of vegetables. It causes wind and flatulence, it is unwholesome and indigestible." The Shah looked at him in astonishment and said, "Didn't you tell me yesterday that the aubergine was an excellent vegetable? How have you come to change your mind?" "Your Majesty," replied the chamberlain, "I am the servant of the Shah, not of the aubergine. Yesterday Your Majesty praised it and so did I; to-day Your Majesty condemned it, and so did I." The proverb is used nowadays of a "sifter of rice", an unprincipled person who turns with every wind that blows.

He winnows wherever the wind is.

Said of an unprincipled person.

I give you advice, and you count flies!

A father was giving his son some advice, and was speaking to him quietly and seriously. But the boy's mind was elsewhere, and his father's words went "in at this ear and out at that". When his father paused, the boy said, "Father, while you were talking I counted twenty flies on our donkey's back!" The father's reply is used proverbially of an inattentive or obstinate person.

Till the calf becomes a cow, its mother's heart will turn to water.

A mother undergoes countless sufferings to raise her child. The proverb is also used more widely to imply that, no matter what you do, a foolish person can never be expected to improve; "the camel's tail will reach the ground" before that will happen.

The rod is sent from Heaven.

Only a green stick will tame the ox and the ass.

Spare the rod and spoil the child. Only fear of punishment will make people do their duty.

An egg-thief becomes a camel-thief.

A small boy stole some eggs from his neighbour and brought them to his mother. Instead of scolding him, she took the eggs and cooked them for dinner. The same thing happened again and again, until egg-stealing became second nature with the boy. By the time he was a grown man, he went still further and stole a camel. But this time he was caught and haled before the *qazi*, who ordered his hand to be cut off. The boy cried out in distress, " You should cut off my mother's hand," and he told the whole story. The *qazi* thereupon pardoned him and, sending for his mother, reprimanded her severely. The proverb indicates that a bad habit will grow worse if it is not checked at once.

Drunkenness brings truth.

A man who is off his guard gives himself away.

You can't hide a drum under a blanket.

Shall I believe your oath or the tail of the cock?

A man stole a cock and hid it under his coat. The owner caught up with him and asked, " What are you doing with my cock? " The thief began to swear that he had never touched the cock, but the owner, looking at the cock's tail protruding from the man's coat, said, " Shall I believe your oath or the tail of the cock? " The moral, like that of the preceding proverb, is that it is useless to conceal crime that is obvious.

He cries to the Shah before the beating.

A man was summoned by the Shah, and before he had even entered the court he began to shout and cry for mercy, saying, " Overlook my offence! Don't beat me!" In fact the Shah had only summoned him for questioning, but by his actions the man revealed his guilt.

Words but not wind.

Words are man's cud.

Men talk when they have nothing else to do.

Words bring words, as wind brings snow.

A red tongue will destroy a green head.

An unruly tongue endangers the whole body.

What is in the pot will come out in the ladle.

What the heart thinks the tongue will say.

Reticence is a sign of wisdom.

Don't answer until you are questioned.

He who talks of others will talk of you.

Beware of gossip-mongers. Compare :

You can shut the city gate, but you can't shut the mouth of men.

We have neither cash for a thief to steal, nor faith for the Devil to steal.

The man who has no ass has no cares over barley and straw.

Two proverbs used to excuse or justify laziness and improvidence, and the shirking of responsibility. Compare :

The larger a man's roof, the more snow it collects.

The bigger a man's head, the worse his headache.

They don't steal a saddle from a bare-back ass.
A penniless man has nothing to lose.

Even the Emam Reza's sheep will not pasture before noon.

The Lady Fatima takes care of slovenly women.
A certain merchant, who had two wives, went on a journey. The elder of the two wives made great preparations for his return, embroidering a beautiful coat of silk and preparing delicious food ; but she neglected to wash her face or tidy herself. The younger wife's present was a coat of the coarsest cloth, and she did no more than sweep the dirt into a corner of the room ; but she took great care with her clothes and her appearance. So the merchant valued her gift as much as the other, and showed it by wearing each in turn.

He placed a bone inside the wound.
A rich man who had injured his leg was taken to an avaricious surgeon, who bound up his wounds and ordered him to be brought regularly for attention. The injured man continued thus in great pain for a long time, until one day the surgeon himself fell sick, and his son took charge of the practice. The son examined the rich man's wound and saw at once that a small piece of bone had lodged inside it. Once this was removed, the wound healed readily. On the surgeon's return, his son told him how he had cured the injured leg, whereupon his father began to abuse him. "Do you suppose I didn't know that bone was there? I put it there myself so that I might profit for a long time from this rich man's wealth. But now in one day you have thrown away our 'nine-gallon cow'." The proverb is used of someone who deliberately spins out a task for reasons of his own.

We did our share, but our ancestor let us down.

A rich man fell sick, and his wife, on the advice of her neighbour, consulted a certain holy man who would, for a suitable sum, pray to his sainted ancestor to restore her husband's health. The saint's prayers however had no effect, since the next morning the rich man died. After the mourning was over the widow met the holy man in the street and reproached him, saying, " That was a fine prayer that you prayed! My husband died the next day." The holy man replied, " I did my share, but my ancestor let me down." The proverb is used as an excuse for failing to carry out a task.

Where was your flask for me to fill with oil?

A certain man was travelling with two vats of oil, and had to go through a pass that was generally frequented by robbers. At the far end of the pass was a shrine, and the traveller, before entering the dangerous spot, prayed to the saint, saying, " If I reach your shrine in safety, I will dedicate some of this oil to you." It so happened that on this occasion there were no robbers in the pass, and by the time he reached the shrine the man had regretted his oath, and making various excuses he continued his journey without leaving any of the oil. A few miles further on his donkey stumbled and fell, and both the vats were broken. The traveller, supposing this to be the retribution of the saint, cried out in querulous protest, " Where was your flask for me to fill?" Like those that precede and follow, this proverb is used in reference to someone who makes unreasonable excuses.

He has sown millet on his rope.

A neighbour came to borrow a rope from Molla Nasr ad-Din. The *molla* went to look for it, but came back and apologized, explaining, " My wife has sown millet on the rope." " What do you mean?" exclaimed the neighbour. " How can you sow millet on a rope?" " Never you mind," retorted the *molla*, " if I don't want to lend it I can say that my wife has sown flour on it if I like!"

He's as bad as Ali the Fault-finder.

A certain young man drove his wife to distraction by his constant fault-finding. One day she devised a plan to forestall all criticism, by arranging everything in two different ways. So when Ali came home and complained, " Why isn't the front-door shut ? " she replied, " One leaf is shut." " Well, it ought to be open." " The other leaf is open." " Well, why have you cleaned the house ? " grumbled Ali. " That half is unswept," replied his wife. " I told you to pencil your eyebrows." " I've done this one," she answered. " Why haven't you combed your hair ? " " I've combed this side." " Well, I told you not to paint your cheeks." " But I haven't painted this one." So it went on all evening ; whether he complained about the food, or the drink, or anything else, she always had an answer for him. At last he lost his temper and in sheer exasperation cried, " Well, why haven't you swept under my moustache ? " The poor wife remained dumb with mortification, for this was the one thing she had never thought of !

8. HONESTY AND FRIENDSHIP

Of an untrustworthy man it will be said that " he hasn't a sound gut in his stomach ", " his henna has no colour ", he is " gravel in one's shoe ". He will delude you with false promises, by " showing you greenery in the garden " or by " giving you a rabbit's dreams " ; he will acquire influence over you by " grasping the vein of your sleep ". He will " reverse his horseshoes " in order to deceive you, as the Turcoman brigands used to do after a successful raid in order to mislead pursuers. Another person to be despised is the hypocrite, the prude, the man who " sprinkles water on a prayer-carpet ". On the reverse side of the picture the proverbs praise harmony and friendship, loyalty, hospitality, generosity and gratitude.

It is easier to make a promise than to fulfil it.

We three have done our part, now you shake your beard.

One night Shah Abbas disguised himself as a dervish and wandered through the streets of Isfahan. On his way he met three robbers, who asked him to join them. It was a very dark night, so dark that " one eye could not see another ". As they walked, they began to boast to one another of their peculiar skills. The first robber said, " If I meet a man but once on a pitch-black night, no matter what he is wearing, I shall recognize him the moment I see him again." The second said, " Any lock that I touch, no matter how strong it is, will open of its own accord." The third said, " I can understand the language of the animals and interpret whatever they say." The false dervish said, " With a shake of my beard I can free any criminal, no matter how guilty he may be." Just then a dog barked, and the third robber, challenged by his comrades, said, " He is saying that, wherever we go to steal, the owner will be with us." The robbers laughed, and continued on their way until they came to the royal treasury. While they were planning to break in, the dervish said, " This is a dangerous task. If the guards wake and catch us, the least that will happen to us is a sound beating." "Don't be scared," retorted the robbers, "we're so experienced in these matters that 'even a *jenn* couldn't get near us', let alone the Shah and his men." Then the robbers scaled the wall and found their way to the strong-room ; the thief who was skilled at locks opened the door at a touch, as he had promised, and the three thieves returned to the waiting dervish with sacks stuffed full of gold and jewels. These they buried outside the city, planning to return and divide them the following morning. The Shah then hastened back to the palace, and there gave orders for the recovery of the stolen goods and the immediate arrest of the thieves. The next morning they were brought before him, and the Shah, addressing them in a tone of thunder, sent for the executioner. But the first robber said, "Your Majesty, four of us were engaged in that robbery. Three of us have done our part ; now let the fourth shake his beard." Shah Abbas, acknowledging that the first robber, by recognizing him, had, like the other two, fulfilled his claim, pardoned the three men and gave them posts at the palace. The proverb is now used when two people agree to carry out a task jointly, and one of them fails in his undertaking.

These are like Solomon's promises to the frogs.

One day the frogs presented a petition to King Solomon, saying, "O Prophet of God! We are naked and destitute ; in winter we freeze with cold, and in summer we roast with heat. Give us a cloak to protect us from the cold of winter and the heat of summer alike." Solomon pleased them with ready promises, but every day thereafter they gathered before him crying, "Our cloak! Our cloak!" and received no satisfaction. So it is that to this very day you may hear the frogs crying, "Our cloak! Our cloak!" The proverb is used of someone who is known to be unreliable in carrying out his promises.

Make it any colour you like but that one!

A man gave a coat to a dyer to be dyed blue. But the next day, when he came for it, the dyer said, " Blue is an unlucky colour, for it is the colour of mourning. Let me dye your coat another colour." The customer agreed, but every day the dyer had a fresh reason for suggesting another colour. Finally the exasperated customer exclaimed, " Give me back the coat undyed ; a simple coat can't take a hundred thousand colours." The dyer, who had sold it the first day, was forced to confess, " I dipped your coat in the vat of oblivion and it took the colour of non-existence." The customer retorted, " You could have made it any colour you liked but that one ! " The proverb is addressed to someone who makes a foolish excuse to conceal his failure to carry out a promise.

The fox produces his tail as a witness.

This proverb is used of someone who produces in support of his claims a witness who, because of a personal interest in the case, is even less reliable than the complainant.

He will make a hundred jugs without a handle.

He will make a hundred knives without a haft.

Both proverbs mean that you can't believe a word he says.

They'd have got me too, if I hadn't been quick.

Two men and a woman plotted to rob Molla Nasr ad-Din of the cow and donkey he was taking to market. First one of the men crept up behind him and cut the cow loose from its leading string without the *molla* noticing. A few minutes later the second man accosted Molla Nasr ad-Din. " Why, *molla*, haven't you noticed? They've stolen your cow. I saw the thieves just now beyond that hill." " Then I'll go and look for them if you'll please hold my donkey." The *molla* searched for a long time, and at last came back empty-handed to the same spot, to find that his ass had gone too. Much upset, he started for home, and saw a woman weeping by the side of a well. " What shall I do ? " she wailed. " I've dropped my earring down this well." "I'll get it for you," exclaimed the gallant *molla*, and stripping off his clothes he climbed down the well. Once again he searched fruitlessly, and clambered to the top to find the woman gone with all his clothes. He picked up his stick and, whirling it round his head, set off at full speed for home. His family greeted him with astonishment, but he retorted, "Don't say a word, for the thieves would have got me too if I hadn't been quick!" The proverb is now used by someone who has fallen victim to trickery.

He reckons like Haji Hadi the coal-merchant.

A Lori tribesman brought a load of charcoal to a coal-merchant in Isfahan. The merchant, Haji Hadi, weighed it, and then began to reckon as follows. "Your charcoal weighed a hundred 'fifties',[1] right? That makes a hundred and fifty, right? So a hundred and fifty from half a *maund* leaves fifty owing to me!" The Lor scratched his head, but couldn't see any flaw in the account. "You must be right," he said, "but what do I get out of it?" The proverb is now used of a dishonest trader.

Under his cup is a saucer.

Wheels within wheels. There is more in this than meets the eye.

The quick-witted die young.

A warning to someone who tries to be too clever.

They tripped him with a melon-skin.

A certain wealthy amir, who enjoyed good living, lavished all his favours upon a particular dancing-girl in his troupe, to the great discontent of the other girls. Try as they might, they could find no way to dislodge her from the amir's affections. But one night they took advantage of the amir's drunkenness to slip a melon-skin under

[1] In Isfahan a *maund* (see Glossary) consists of four *charaks*, each of fifty units, and so often known as "fifty".

her feet as she was dancing. She fell heavily and injured her leg, and by the time she was able to dance again, the amir was no longer interested in her. The proverb is used of someone who has been duped or made a victim of his own conceit.

The quarrel was over the molla's *quilt.*

One night a fight started outside Molla Nasr ad-Din's house. He got up, wrapped his quilt round his shoulders, and went to investigate. As soon as the rowdies saw him, they snatched his quilt and ran off down the road. The *molla* went quietly back to bed. " What was the matter ? " asked his wife. " Nothing," said Molla Nasr ad-Din, " the whole quarrel was over the *molla's* quilt. Once they had that, they made no more trouble." The proverb is used when someone is deluded by a mock quarrel or some similar deception. A wise man in such a case " hangs on to his quilt with both hands ".

Our turn to dance will come.

A camel and a donkey were turned loose from a caravan because they were too exhausted to travel any longer. However, as luck would have it, they found a valley with excellent pasture, and there they lived comfortably for a long time. One day a caravan passed in the distance, and when the donkey heard the bells, he began to bray. " Be quiet," said the camel, " they'll hear us and catch us, and we shall be taken from this fine place." " I can't help it," answered the donkey, " I feel like singing." The muleteers of the caravan soon came up, seized both the animals, and took them along with the caravan. Before long they came to a deep river and, as the donkey could not cross it by himself, they lifted him on to the camel's back. In the middle of the river the camel suddenly started to kick. " Keep still," cried the donkey, " you'll throw me into the river." " I can't help it," retorted the camel, " I feel like dancing, and now it's my turn." And without more ado he threw the donkey off his back and left him to drown. The proverb is used by someone as a warning to a man who has cheated him.

A crooked load will not last the journey.
Dishonest practices will get you nowhere.

The snake must be straight to enter the hole.
Honesty is the best policy.

" Praise God" never made any one fat.

" Praise God" never dyed anyone's coat.
Don't be deceived by hypocrisy.

Hood and cloak do not make the dervish.
A man must not be judged by his outward appearance.

Don't bandage a head that doesn't ache.
Don't be a hypocrite in order to gain sympathy.

Don't be duped by the praying of the hermit's cat.
Shah Shoja', fourteenth-century ruler of Shiraz, had a great opinion of a hermit named Emad, who maintained his reputation by a variety of tricks, of which his most noteworthy was that he had trained his cat to stand behind him when he prayed and imitate him. Shah Shoja' took this as evidence of the hermit's piety, but the poet Hafez satirized Emad in a lyric ending with the above line. This so incensed the hermit that, when he came across a verse by Hafez that could be interpreted as blasphemy, he took it straight to the Shah. On hearing of this, Hafez hastily composed another verse putting the blasphemous verse into the mouth of a Christian, and thus absolved himself from blame, since the reporting of blasphemy could not be held to be blasphemy. The proverb serves to warn one against hypocrites and deceivers.

" Halva, halva" does not sweeten the mouth.
Compare " fine words butter no parsnips ".

My new sleeve should eat the polou*!*

One day Molla Nasr ad-Din went to dine at a certain house, but since he was wearing his old clothes, he was put at the foot of the cloth near the door, and every other guest who came was seated above him. The next time he went to that house, he wore his best clothes; and when he entered and was about to sit in his former place, the whole gathering rose to their feet in protest and insisted that he sit at the head of the cloth next to the host. Soon a large dish of *polou* was brought in, and the *molla*, helping himself liberally, proceeded to put it into his sleeve, saying, "My new sleeve should eat the *polou*!" The proverb is used when people pay more attention to outward appearance than to inward qualities.

Salt seasons tainted meat, but what if the salt is tainted?

The Arabs have a proverb, "If the teacher be corrupt, the world will be corrupt."

You cannot clap with one hand.

Two heads are better than one.

When the cat and mouse agree, the grocer is ruined.

The patriotic poet Iraj Mirza used this proverb in a satirical poem on the Anglo-Russian Agreement of 1907 dividing Persia into spheres of influence.

Who is lost from sight is lost from the heart.

Distance preserves friendship.

Two contrasting proverbs that may be compared with "Out of sight, out of mind" and "Absence makes the heart grow fonder."

A wise enemy is better than a foolish friend.

This widely used proverb comes from Rumi's *Masnavi*, where the following story is told. A wise man was riding along a road, when he saw a snake crawling into the mouth of a sleeping man. Too late to stop it, he seized a club and began to beat the unfortunate sleeper. The man leapt up, but the rider continued to beat him and drove him to a tree where a quantity of rotten apples were lying on the ground. These he proceeded to cram into his mouth, regardless of his protests and abuse. Then he continued beating him unmercifully until at last the wretched man vomited and brought up the snake. As soon as he saw it, the man fell on his knees and began to praise the rider whom he had just been abusing. "But why," he said, "didn't you wake me first and warn me?" "If I had done that," replied his rescuer, "you would have died of fright on the spot. You would never have had the strength even to vomit."

Heart finds a way to heart.

Love and friendship are always mutual.

A head without love is like a marrow-plant without fruit.

Sheikh Baha'i wrote, "The breast that has no love for the fair is like a sack full of old bones."

For one guest the host will kill a cow.

If one counts on the generosity of others, one will not be disappointed.

The guest is the host's donkey.

The guest must be content with what the host provides. Ferdousi has a line in the *Shahnamé*, "In his own palace the host is king."

Don't break your host's salt-cellar.

Don't look a gift-horse in the mouth. Salt is regarded as the symbol of hospitality. The Persians also say:

Don't count the teeth of a gift-horse.

Hospitality is two-sided.

One good turn deserves another. Compare :

The neighbour's bowl has two feet.

See that your bowl brings back a pot.

This proverb, which has the meaning of " One good turn deserves another," may be connected with the Molla Nasr ad-Din story on page 50.

A grateful dog is better than an ungrateful man.

" Sackcloth " even to me ?

A debtor was brought by his creditors before the *qazi*, and his lawyer privately instructed him to answer the single word " sackcloth " to any and every question that he was asked. In this way the *qazi* and the creditors were soon convinced that he had been driven out of his mind by his worries, and they let him go. The next day the triumphant lawyer came to collect his fee, and was greeted with the single word " sackcloth ". The expression is used in protest against gross ingratitude.

The reward of good is evil.

A rider discovered a snake caught in the midst of a forest fire. When the snake saw him, it appealed for help, and since the rider was a God-fearing man, he overcame his fears and, holding out his saddle-bag on the end of a spear, lifted the snake out of the fire. " Now go where you will," he said, " and in gratitude for your release trouble mankind no more." But the snake turned on him, saying, " I shall not leave till I have killed you and your camel. You knew that I was a symbol of evil to men, and yet you ignored the proverb, ' Kindness to evil men is like injury to good men.' So you must take the consequences. Moreover, I am only copying the practice of men themselves. ' You will now buy in a moment what you sell all year.' "

The rider protested and said, " If you can prove to me that this is the practice of men, I will accept my fate." Just then a buffalo appeared, and the snake asked him, " What is the reward of good?" The buffalo answered, " According to the practice of men it is evil. Every year I raised calves for my master and gave him milk and butter, but now that I am old he plans to sell me to the butcher." The snake turned triumphantly to the rider, but the latter said, " According to law one witness is not enough." So the snake turned to a tree and asked, " What is the reward of good?" The tree replied, " According to the practice of men it is evil. I give shade and rest to weary travellers, and then they tear off my branches to make shafts for axe and spade." The snake turned once more in triumph to the rider, but the latter said, " Life is dear to me. I beg you, find yet one more witness to support you, and then I will submit without question to my fate." The snake then noticed a fox who had been listening to the conversation, but before the question could be put to him, the fox cried out, " Of course the reward of good is evil. Now tell me, what good has the man done to the snake that he should be rewarded with evil?" The man told his story, and the fox asked the snake if he agreed. " Yes," was the reply, " and here is the bag in which he lifted me." " How ridiculous!" said the fox: " How could a huge snake like you get into that tiny bag?" " I'll show you," replied the snake, and slid back into the bag. The fox cried out, " When you find your enemy in bonds, don't release him," and the rider, hastily closing the opening, beat the bag on the ground until the snake was dead. The proverb is now used when someone returns evil for good.

He whose hand is severed knows the worth of a severed hand.

A thief was sentenced to have his hand cut off. He made not the slightest complaint, but picked up his hand and went on his way. A little way off, however, he met another thief who had suffered a similar penalty, and at once he began to weep and wail. " Why are you crying now," they asked him, " when you didn't even murmur before?" " There was no one who could appreciate my loss," replied the thief, " but this man is able to sympathize with me." A similar proverb says :

He whose harvest is burnt knows the worth of a burnt harvest.

The tooth hurts the body, the tongue hurts the soul.

One's own pains are slight when the neighbour knocks.

One should sacrifice one's self in order to help others.

He has no gruel for himself, but he takes stew to his neighbour.

Said of a generous and unselfish man.

9. *MAN'S TRUE WORTH*

A man's true worth lies in his inward qualities, not in his outward appearance. Only the heart of the guilty " boils like garlic and vinegar ", only those who have something to conceal need to " keep their face red with slapping ", that is to say, keep up appearances. It is true that bad company may corrupt a man, but he who is bad at heart will be " better known than the unbelief of the Devil ". " Even his dog is better than he is." He will be recognized by his actions, no matter how he may try to hide the truth. On the other hand, the wise and experienced man will always be respected ; " his hat is worthy of his head ".

An innocent man goes only to the foot of the gallows.

Gold in its purity fears nothing from the earth.

He whose account is clear need have no fear of the day of reckoning.

The liar is forgetful.

The liar shames himself.

The thieving cat runs when you pick up a stick.

A guilty man is always anxious and fearful.

When the pot is open, the cat forgets its manners.

When the mosque is open, the dog forgets its manners.

An habitual wrongdoer readily succumbs to temptation.

A false lamp gives no light.

A rotten aubergine gets no disease.

A worthless person cannot get any worse.

A mean man is vile company.

A line from a poem by Hafez, in which he complains of the boredom of drinking without his beloved.

Virtuous company makes you virtuous.

At night the cat is the same as the sable.

At night the ass's foal is the same as the peacock.

At night a cotton-seed is the same as a pearl.

Three proverbs comparable with the French "La nuit tous les chats sont gris."

Two donkeys together will act alike and smell alike.

A man is known by the company he keeps.

Pigeon flies with pigeon, hawk with hawk.

This verse from Nezami compares with Farrokhi's line :

The muleteer goes to the camel-driver's house.

That is to say, birds of a feather flock together.

Everything reverts to its origin.

It is useless for a man to pretend to be other than what he is. A hermit by his magic turned a mouse into a beautiful girl, and wished to give her in marriage. "I will marry the strongest person in the world," she said. So the hermit offered her to the sun, but the sun said, "The cloud is stronger than me, for he can hide me from the eyes of men." The hermit went to the cloud, but the cloud said, "The wind is stronger than me, for he can blow me where he wishes." So the hermit went to the wind, but the wind said, "The mountain is stronger than me, for he always stands firm against me." So the hermit went to the mountain, but the mountain said, "The mouse is stronger than me, for he can burrow deep into my heart." So the hermit went to the mouse, but the mouse said, "I will only marry someone of my own kind." So after all the hermit was obliged to change the girl back into her original form.

The leek springs from its seed and Hasan from his father.

Like father, like son.

The wolf-cub becomes a wolf, though it be raised among men.

A verse from the *Golestan* of Sa'di.

A beggar's child is always a beggar's child.

A king was passing through the streets of his capital, when he observed a beautiful girl begging by the roadside. He gave orders that she should be taken to his *andarun* and there trained and educated in all the arts and graces by the most skilled teachers. Owing to her natural intelligence she progressed rapidly, and after a year of such teaching she was so beautiful and accomplished that the king decided to take her for his wife. The girl agreed on the one condition that she should always take her meals alone. The king agreed to this condition, and the wedding duly took place. Nevertheless, the king was not long able to restrain his curiosity over the fact that, when meal-time came, she had the food served in her own room, and would not touch it until the servants had gone and she had locked the door. Determined to probe the mystery, he instructed an old nurse to hide herself in the girl's room and to report to him what happened. She observed that, as soon as the door was locked, the girl took each of the dishes and placed them in different corners of the room. Then she stood in front of each in turn and, in the whining tone of a beggar, said, " In the name of God, spare a morsel ! " She then took a mouthful, swallowed it greedily, and passed on to the next dish, where she repeated the performance. When she was finally satisfied, she put the dishes back on the cloth and unlocked the door. When the king heard this story, he was amazed, and observed, " The child of a beggar is always the child of a beggar ! "

Nature, not spite, gives the scorpion its sting.

A tortoise and a scorpion were close friends. One day they set out to look for a new home, and on their way came to a broad river. " How shall I cross this ? " exclaimed the scorpion. " Don't worry," replied the tortoise, " I will carry you safely across on my back." When they were half-way across, the tortoise heard the scorpion moving about, and asked him what he was doing. " I am trying out my sting on your shell," he replied. " You ungrateful wretch ! " exclaimed the tortoise. " It is true that your sting can never pierce my shell, but is this the way to repay me for risking my life for you ? " " Forgive me," replied the scorpion, " but my nature requires that I should sting, whether it be the back of a friend or the breast of an enemy." This story is from the *Anvar-e Soheili.*

The repentance of the wolf is death.

The leopard cannot change his spots.

If the rustic's a governor, the bear's Avicenna.

You can't make a silk purse out of a sow's ear.

Every flower has its scent.

Everyone is not driven with the same stick.

What is in the pot will leak from it.

You won't find fruit on a willow-tree.

Vinegar drips from the vinegar-jar.

A snake rears snakes.

The last four proverbs resemble "A tree is known by its fruit."

The handful is a sample of the donkey-load.

A seeing eye is better than three hundred sticks.

Seek the truth from a child.

A child may hit the target in error.

"Out of the mouths of babes and sucklings . . ." The *Golestan* tells how a king was out hunting and placed his ring upon the top of a ruined dome. "This ring to him who shoots an arrow through it!" he cried. Four hundred archers tried and failed. A child was playing on a neighbouring roof with a toy bow and arrow, and by chance the wind caught his arrow and carried it through the ring. The king praised him highly and gave him the ring; but the boy took his bow and arrow and burnt them, "for thus," he said, "its first success will remain unspoiled".

Ripeness is in wisdom, not in years.

Youth is too wild to worship God, and age too weak.

This line is from Ansari. Attar wrote:

Once I had strength but no wisdom; now I have wisdom but no strength.

To a wise man a nod is enough.

If anyone is at home, a word is enough.

One stroke is enough for a noble horse.

He who has knowledge has power.

This verse comes from the opening lines of Ferdousi's *Shahnamé*, and is now used as the motto of the Persian Ministry of Education.

Reasoned words have no answer.

One wise man is a hat for a hundred bald heads, and a stick for a hundred blind men.

The Lord Ali knows where to lead the camel.

A Shi'ite and a Sunnite were disputing. The Shi'ite said, " On the Day of Resurrection Ali will go to Heaven and Omar to Hell." " You are wrong," said the Sunnite. " On the Day of Resurrection Omar will mount a camel, and Ali will go on foot and lead it to Heaven." " If Ali is the camel-driver," retorted the Shi'ite, " he will know where to lead it." The proverb is used to express confidence in one's own ability to perform a task ; " leave it to me, and nothing will go wrong ". For the Shi'ite and Sunnite views of Ali and Omar, see the Glossary.

Don't go to the doctor, go to the man who knows.

Still waters become stagnant.

The kabob must be turned to cook.

Both proverbs imply that travel is necessary for a man to gain wisdom and experience. The Koran says, " Travel through the earth and observe the fate of those before you" (xxx. 41). Many Persian poets have written on this theme, and Anvari's line among others has become proverbial :

Travel ripens a man.

They have killed the camel.
All is over.

BIBLIOGRAPHY

Ali Akbar Dehkhodâ, *Amsâl va Hekam* (Proverbs and Sayings), 4 vols., Tehran, 1931.

Amir Qoli Amini, *Dâstânhâ-e Amsâl* (Proverbial Tales), 2 vols., Isfahan, 1945.

Yusef Rahmati, *Farhang-e Âmmiyâné* (Colloquial Dictionary), Tehran, 1951.

Abbâs Mohtashem Nuri, *Amsâl-e Englisi be-Fârsi* (English Proverbs in Persian), Tehran, 1944.

Sobhi Mohtadi, *Afsânéhâ-e Kohan* (Old Fables), Tehran, 1949.

D. C. Phillott, *Persian Saws and Proverbs* (Memoirs of the Asiatic Society of Bengal, Vol. I, No. 15, pp. 302–37), Calcutta, 1906.

J. L. Burckhardt, *Arabic Proverbs*, London, 1930.

Carlo Landberg, *Proverbes et Dictons du Peuple Arabe* (Vol. I), Leiden, 1883.

Ahmad Taimur Pāshā, *al-Amthāl al-'āmmīya* (Popular Proverbs), Cairo, 1949.

E. J. Davis, *Osmanli Proverbs and Quaint Sayings*, London, 1898.

Aesop's Fables, a new version by the Rev. Thomas James, M.A., London, 1848.

Bess Allen Donaldson, *The Wild Rue*, a study of Muhammadan magic and folklore in Iran, London, 1938.

D. L. R. and E. O. Lorimer, *Persian Tales*, London, 1919.

Mashdi Galeen Khanom and L. P. Elwell-Sutton, *The Wonderful Sea-Horse and Other Persian Tales*, London, 1950.

GLOSSARY

(Dates are A.D., unless otherwise stated)

ABBAS, SHAH (reigned 1587–1629), was one of the most famous of the Safavid rulers of Persia, and contemporary of Queen Elizabeth and the Mogul Emperor Akbar, with both of whom he corresponded. During his reign Persian art and architecture reached new heights, and his capital at Isfahan became renowned in Europe from the descriptions of the many travellers who visited it.

ALI, the son-in-law of the Prophet Muhammad through his marriage to the latter's daughter Fatima, is revered throughout the Shi'ite world, sometimes even more than the Prophet himself. He was assassinated in 656. See the note on Shi'ism.

ALVAND (12,290 ft.) is situated some forty miles south of Hamadan, in western Persia.

ANDARUN : the inner part of a Persian house, reserved for the womenfolk and the closest male relatives.

ANSARI (1006–88) was born in Herat, and was one of the earlier Persian mystical poets.

ANUSHIRVAN (reigned 531–78) is known to history as " the Just ". One of the later Sasanid rulers of Persia, he is remembered for his successful campaigns against the Roman Empire and for his reorganization of the country's administration, finances and agriculture.

ANVAR-E SOHEILI : a somewhat ornate version of the book of *Kalilé va Demné* (q.v.), composed by the theologian Hosein Va'ez-e Kashefi in the fifteenth century.

ANVARI (twelfth century) spent most of his life in Merv and Balkh in Turkestan, and is generally regarded as one of the greatest of the Persian poets.

ASADI (eleventh century) is chiefly known for his epic poem, the *Garshasp-namé*, and for his Persian lexicon.

ASHRAFI : a gold coin of the eighteenth century, equivalent to a sovereign.

ATTAR (d. *c.* 1230) was one of the greatest of the Persian mystical poets, among his best known works being the *Mantiq at-Tair* (the Language of the Birds).

AVICENNA, more correctly known as Abu Ali ibn Sina, was born about 980 and died in 1037. Equally famous as philosopher and physician, he was one of those who carried on the tradition of Greece and transmitted it to the Islamic world and Europe.

BAKHTIYARI : a large tribe occupying the mountainous area between Isfahan and the head of the Persian Gulf.

BAKU : a city on the western shore of the Caspian Sea in what is now Soviet Azerbaijan. It has been noted for centuries for its oil deposits.

BALKH : a city in Afghanistan near the Russian frontier, it is reputed to be one of the oldest in the world.

BEIZA : a district some twenty-five miles to the north of Shiraz in southern Persia.

BOZORGMEHR : Grand Vizier to Anushirvan (q.v.) and initiator of many of his reforms.

BUSTAN : one of the poetical works of Sa'di.

CHENGIZ KHAN (1162–1227) began his career of world conquest in 1219, and at his death his empire extended from the borders of China to Iraq. His sons and successors swept across Russia into Poland and Hungary. Chengiz' ruthlessness and disregard for human life are proverbial.

DAJJAL : the false Messiah or Antichrist who is to appear before the Day of Resurrection.

DEMNÉ : v. Kalilé va Demné.

DERVISH : a religious mendicant, generally belonging to one of a large number of orders, and distinguished by special costume and appurtenances.

DINAR : one of the smallest units of Persian currency. Formerly one thousand, now one hundred, go to the *rial* (q.v.).

EMAM : according to Shi'ite doctrine the succession to the Prophet was carried on through his lineal descendant, Hosein, son of Ali and Fatima, and his children. These constitute a line of *emams* (some say twelve, some seven), the last of whom is said to have disappeared and will return at the end of the world.

FARROKHI (tenth century), one of the first great poets of Moslem Persia.

FATIMA, daughter of the Prophet Muhammad (he had no surviving male progeny), married one of his early adherents, Ali (q.v.).

FERDOUSI (932–1020), Persia's greatest epic poet, wrote the *Shahnamé* (Book of Kings), containing in some 60,000 couplets the legendary history of Persia from the earliest times to the Arab conquest.

GHAZNÉ: a city in Afghanistan, about a hundred miles south-west of Kabul, and at one time the capital of Soltan Mahmud (q.v.).

GOLESTAN: the most famous of Sa'di's works, containing anecdotes in prose and verse covering every aspect of life.

HAFEZ (d. 1389) spent his whole life in Shiraz, and is considered to be Persia's greatest lyric poet. His poetry may be interpreted literally or mystically, and his *Divan* (Collected Poems) is popularly used for the taking of auguries.

HALVA: a sweetmeat composed of flour, butter and sugar.

HATEM TA'I: a legendary Arab chief celebrated in pre-Islamic poetry for his generosity.

HOSEIN: the younger son of Ali, son-in-law of the Prophet, he was killed at the battle of Kerbela in 680, an event that is still mourned annually throughout the Shi'ite world.

HURI: one of the beautiful maidens who will minister to the faithful in Paradise.

IRAJ MIRZA (1874–1925), a prince of the Qajar dynasty that ruled Persia during the nineteenth century, is remembered for his patriotic and satirical poetry, and for his progressive ideas.

ISFAHAN: the second largest city in Persia, and formerly the capital. It has long been a centre of industry and craft, and owes much of its beauty to Shah Abbas (q.v.).

JAMI (1414–92), one of the last great Persian poets, was famous also as a mystic and a scholar.

JERJIS: St. George, who is included by Islam among the prophets.

JENN: spirits said to be present everywhere, and generally ill-disposed or at any rate in need of propitiation.

KABOB : a cube of meat threaded on to a skewer or spit and roasted over a charcoal brazier.

KALILÉ VA DEMNÉ : a Persian version of the Fables of Bidpai or Pilpai, translated by Nasrollah of Ghazné in the middle of the twelfth century from the Arabic of Ibn al-Muqaffa', who himself translated it from the Pahlavi in about 750. The Pahlavi translation was made during the reign of Anushirvan from the original Sanskrit, but is no longer extant.

KEI KAVUS : a legendary king of Persia, possibly to be identified with the Median king Cyaxares (633–584 B.C.).

KERBELA : a holy city in Iraq, 100 miles south of Baghdad, and the scene of the death of Hosein (q.v.) in 680.

KERMAN : a city in south-eastern Persia, 300 miles west of Shiraz.

KHONSAR : a town in central Persia, 100 miles north-west of Isfahan.

KURD : a tribe occupying the western and north-western areas of Persia. Many Kurds are also to be found in Iraq, Turkey and Syria.

LEILA : the heroine of a famous love-story, treated by Nezami and other poets. Like Juliet, she was forbidden by her family to see her lover, who as a result lost his reason—whence his name Majnun (q.v.)—and wandered into the desert. Leila followed him, but was caught by her own people before she could save him.

LOR : a tribe occupying the western areas of Persia, between the Kurds and the Bakhtiyaris (q.v.).

MAHMUD, SOLTAN (reigned 998–1030) : had his capital at Ghazné, and conquered much of Persia, India and other lands. He also patronized many of the famous men of letters of the time.

MAJNUN : the " maddened one ", hero of the story of Leila and Majnun (v. Leila).

MASNAVI : strictly speaking, any poem composed in rhymed couplet form ; the name is especially applied to the great allegorical poem of Jalal ad-Din Rumi (q.v.).

MAS'UD SA'D SALMAN (d. 1121 or 1131) was an early poet of distinction.

MAUND : a weight varying in different parts of Persia from six to twelve pounds, the latter in Isfahan.

MAZANDARAN : a province of Persia bordering the southern and south-eastern shores of the Caspian Sea.

MOHARRAM : the first month of the Moslem (lunar) year, and the month in which Hosein was killed at Kerbela. His death is still re-enacted during this month by pious Shi'ites.

MOLLA : a Shi'ite religious dignitary corresponding as nearly as may be to the village priest (though no priesthood as such exists in Islam).

NADER SHAH (reigned 1736–47) united Persia for a brief period, and extended his conquests into India.

NASER AD-DIN SHAH (reigned 1848–96), the fourth ruler of the Qajar dynasty, was the first reigning Shah of Persia to visit Europe—in 1873, 1878 and 1889.

NASER-E KHOSROU (1004–88), a noted traveller and poet.

NASR AD-DIN, MOLLA : a fictitious comic character, about whom many stories are told illustrating rustic simplicity and logic. In Turkey he is known as Hoca Nasrettin, and in Egypt as Goha.

NEZAMI (1141–1203), one of Persia's greatest mystical and romantic poets, was born in Ganjé, in what is now Soviet Azerbaijan.

OMAR : the second of the Orthodox Caliphs, or successors of the Prophet Muhammad. He is not recognized by the Shi'ites, who execrate his name.

POLOU : a dish of rice, vegetables, chopped meat or chicken, etc.

QAZI : a magistrate responsible for administering the Islamic law, by which all justice was guided until recent times.

REZA, EMAM (d. 816): the eighth of the Emams according to the orthodox branch of the Shi'ites, who recognize twelve in all. He is buried in Mashhad, in the north-east of Persia, where his shrine is next in importance to Kerbela as a place of pilgrimage.

RIAL : a coin worth at present about 1½*d*., but considerably more in earlier times. The name is derived from the Spanish *real*.

ROSTAM : a legendary Persian hero. The story of his fight with his son Sohrab is told in brief on page 31, and is known to the English-speaking world through the version by Matthew Arnold.

RUMI, JALAL AD-DIN (1207–73), possibly the most famous and revered of all Persia's mystical poets. His monumental *Masnavi* is sometimes known as the "Persian Koran".

SABZEVAR : a town in the north-east of Persia, about 150 miles west of Mashhad.

SA'DI (1184–1291) travelled widely during his lifetime, falling captive to the Crusaders at one time, and returned in his old age to his native town of Shiraz, where he set down in writing his accumulated experience and knowledge.

SAFAR : the second month of the Moslem (lunar) year.

SANA'I (*c.* 1045–1141), one of Persia's most distinguished mystical poets. His best known work is the *Hadiqat al-Haqiqa* (the Garden of Truth).

SAYED : a man claiming descent from the Prophet through his daughter Fatima, and entitled to wear a green sash.

SEDEH : a village near Isfahan, whose inhabitants are noted for their simplicity.

SHAHI : a coin worth half a *rial* (q.v.).

SHAHNAMÉ : the Book of Kings, the great epic poem composed by Ferdousi.

SHEIKH BAHA'I (1546–1622) was born in Syria and came with his father to Persia as refugees from Sunnite persecution. He wrote a number of theological works and poems.

SHEMR : the man held responsible by the Shi'ites for the death of Hosein at Kerbela.

SHI'ISM : Islam divided at an early date into two great sects, the Shi'ites and the Sunnites. The dispute originally arose as one of succession to the Prophet, the Sunnites holding that the Caliphs should be elected, as were the first four, Abu Bakr, Omar, Othman and Ali, while the Shi'ites supported the claims of Ali's sons as the direct descendants of the Prophet through his daughter Fatima. The dispute flared up after the death of Othman, when Ali was challenged by Mu'awiya, who established himself as Caliph in Damascus. After Ali's assassination in 656, his sons Hasan and Hosein continued his claim ; the former abdicated in 661, and the latter was slain on the battle-field of Kerbela in 680. Shi'ism subsequently became a vehicle for the discontents of the under-privileged, and for Persian nationalism and religious ideas. Its adherents are now largely concentrated in Persia (where it is the State religion) and Iraq.

SHIRAZ: a city in south Persia, birthplace of Sa'di, Hafez and other famous men.

SHOJA', SHAH (reigned 1357–84), the second of the Mozaffarid dynasty, who ruled over Yazd, Kerman, Shiraz and Kurdistan. He was a patron of the poet Hafez.

SOHRAB: a legendary Persian hero (v. Rostam).

SUNNITE: an adherent of one of the two major divisions in Islam, the other being the Shi'ites (q.v.).

TATAR: a general term for the Turkish and Mongol inhabitants of Central Asia.

TEHRAN: the capital of Persia since 1794. It lies about 100 miles south of the Caspian Sea, from which it is separated by the Elborz Mountains, and has at present a population of about 1,000,000.

TUMAN: a coin equal in value to ten *rials*.

TURAN: the legendary enemy of Iran, and evidently to be identified with the Turks of Central Asia.

TURCOMAN: a name given to the nomadic inhabitants of Turkestan, who in the past frequently raided over the border into the Persian province of Khorasan in the north-east.

VAQF: property administered as a religious endowment or trust, for the upkeep of a mosque or shrine, or in general for the benefit of the poor.

YAZD: a city in south-east Persia, the main centre of the now almost extinct Zoroastrian community of Persia.

ZOLALI (d. 1615), a comparatively undistinguished figure in Persia's more recent literary history.

ZOROASTER: the founder of the ancient religion of Persia, his traditional dates are 660–583 B.C. His teaching included the doctrine of the perpetual conflict between good and evil, between light and darkness—whence the erroneous assumption that it involved sun-worship. Zoroastrianism was largely displaced by Islam (though the Persian form of Shi'ism incorporated many of its doctrines), but it has survived in Yazd and in the Parsi community of Bombay.

Books of similar interest in The Wisdom of the East Series

ARABIC and PERSIAN POETRY

HAFIZ OF SHIRAZ. Thirty Poems translated by PETER AVERY and JOHN HEATH-STUBBS.

THE PERSIAN MYSTICS. The Invocations of Sheikh Abdullāh Ansāri of Herat, A.D. 1005–1090. By SARDAR SIR JOGENDRA SINGH. Foreword by MAHATMA GANDHI.

THE DIWAN OF ABU'L-ALA. By HENRY BAERLEIN.

ARABIC and PERSIAN PHILOSOPHY

AN ARAB PHILOSOPHY OF HISTORY. Selections from the Prolegomena of Ibn Khaldun of Tunis, 1332–1406. Translated by CHARLES ISSAWI, M.A. "Mr. Issawi has earned the gratitude of the English-speaking world by introducing it in admirably translated sections to the work of one of the greatest Arab sages."—*Truth.*

AVICENNA ON THEOLOGY. Translated by PROFESSOR A. J. ARBERRY, Litt.D. "Professor Arberry's little book is a worthy tribute from the Western world to a genius which is truly described as that 'of one of the profoundest and most courageous thinkers in history.'"—*Truth.*

THE SPIRITUAL PHYSICK OF RHAZES. Translated from the Arabic by PROFESSOR A. J. ARBERRY, Litt.D. "The Introduction could hardly be bettered. It tells readers exactly what they want to know, clearly and without a word being wasted, with charm as well as learning."—*Journal of the Royal Central Asian Society.*

THE MYSTERIES OF SELFLESSNESS. By the late SIR MUHAMMAD IQBAL. Translated by PROFESSOR A. J. ARBERRY, Litt.D. " Professor Arberry's admirable translation provides an opportunity to understand something of the Muslim viewpoint."—*Great Britain and the East.*

General Titles in The Wisdom of the East Series

LITERATURES OF THE EAST : An Appreciation. Edited by ERIC B. CEADEL. With an Introduction by PROFESSOR A. J. ARBERRY, Litt.D. " This work is a valuable introduction to the great literature of Asia."—*The Times Literary Supplement.*

EASTERN SCIENCE. An Outline of its Scope and Contribution. By H. J. J. WINTER, Ph.D., M.Sc. " Dr. Winter has proved splendidly equal to the task ; a thoroughly satisfactory work."—*The Times.*

THE GLAD TIDINGS OF BAHA'U'LLAH. Extracts from the Sacred Writings of the Bahá'ís, with an Introduction and Notes by GEORGE TOWNSHEND, M.A. " Enlightened and useful."—*Aryan Path.*

MANIFOLD UNITY. The Ancient World's Perception of the Divine Pattern of Harmony and Compassion. By COLLUM.

ONE IN ALL. An Anthology of Religion from the Sacred Scriptures of the Living Faiths. Compiled by EDITH B. SCHNAPPER, Ph.D. With an Introduction by BARON ERIK PALMSTIERNA. " A thoughtful and judicious selection."—*Aryan Path.*